One Palace, a Thousand Doorways

One Palace, a Thousand Doorways

Songlines Through Bhakti, Sufi, and Baul Oral Traditions

VIPUL RIKHI
with SHABNAM VIRMANI

SPEAKING
TIGER

SPEAKING TIGER PUBLISHING PVT. LTD
4381 / 4, Ansari Road, Daryaganj
New Delhi 110002

First published in paperback by Speaking Tiger 2019

ISBN: 978-93-89231-22-9
eISBN: 978-93-89231-23-6

10 9 8 7 6 5 4 3 2 1

Typeset in Adobe Caslon Pro by SÜRYA, New Delhi
Printed at Sanat Printers, Kundli

dedicated to
the many wonderful folk traditions
of this incredible land

CONTENTS

INTRODUCTION

One palace, a thousand doorways
Countless windows in between
From wherever I look
The Beloved stands before me
—Shah Latif

We stand perhaps at the cusp of a turning point in human history. With politics getting shriller and more abrasive, economics more abstruse and incomprehensible, academics more and more entrenched in its isolation, urbanization and industrial output hitting the limits of their growth, and an incredible burst in the consumption of various media on personal devices, with no clear divide between the 'real' and 'unreal' or 'fake', we can truly say that we have not been here before. This is unprecedented. The planet seems under clear and present danger. Despite all our vaunted 'progress', war and armed conflict are nowhere in retreat. Even as more and more people are able to express widely through various media, we seem increasingly more in disagreement than in understanding. How did we come to this?

This book is not civilizational in its scope. It is personal, in the same vein as the songs and poetry it seeks to expose are personal. But also, in that vein, perhaps the civilizational/universal and the personal/individual are not so far apart. The meaning of human existence at large, and of an individual human life, are not divorced from each other. The songs that flow in this book speak of the two in a single breath. These songs, despite being centuries-old, speak to where we are right now. The oral tradition which carries these songs, its practices and ethos, have a lot to contribute towards understanding and grappling with the present situation.

Oral Traditions of Mystic Poetry

For several centuries, in many parts of what are now India, Pakistan and Bangladesh, have thrived the oral traditions of several mystic poets. Who are the 'mystic poets' and what are these 'oral traditions'? 'Mystic poet' is a term we employ for a range of poets from the Bhakti, Sufi and Baul traditions. The term more commonly used in Hindi and other Indian languages for Bhakti poets is 'saint-poets'. Or, in a parallel tradition, the term 'Sufi poet' is used. Such an epithet would be used for a practicing Sufi, or a 'Sufi saint'. In the Baul tradition, people refer to 'Baul seekers' or 'Baul masters', who were primarily practitioners and additionally poets. So, in a sense, we can see that the term 'mystic poet' refers to an umbrella of poets who are more than poets in a literary sense. It is not only that they speak about esoteric or mystical ideas. It is also that in popular understanding they are held to be 'practitioners' or 'saints' or 'masters', who wrote poetry to express an experienced truth. In other words, their being is commensurate with the truths they seek to express through poetry. It is not speculative knowledge of mysticism being put into verse. It is a poetic expression of a lived truth, or truths.

Many of these poets only spoke or sang. They did not, in the proper sense, write. Kabir himself was unlettered; in typical, confrontational fashion, he celebrated that station. It was not a matter of embarrassment for him.

Never touched ink or paper
Never held a pen in hand
The wisdom of all four ages
Kabir spoke with his tongue

We use the term 'oral traditions' to refer to methods and ways in which the poetry of Kabir and several other poets has survived, and indeed grown, through centuries, in a non-textual form. To put it simply, the poems have survived as songs or sayings / quotations, purely by force of being sung or repeated. They were possibly songs to begin with. Just as the term 'mystic poet' is not used to refer to a poet who merely writes about mysticism, but rather to a mystic who writes, so the songs of the mystics are not primarily written and read, but are sung, heard, repeated, and embodied. The tradition thrives and survives on the basis of oral transmission from one body to another.

In many parts of north and central India, a tradition of singing Kabir and other Bhakti poets such as Gorakhnath, Dharamdas, Meera and others, thrives in the village setting. In the western parts, such as Rajasthan, Punjab and Gujarat (as also in Sindh), this intermixes with the songs of Sufi poets such as Bulleshah, Baba Farid, Shah Latif and others. And on the eastern side, in Bengal (and also in Bangladesh), there is a parallel tradition of singing mystic poets, the most prominent of whom is Lalon Fakir. This tradition is made up of 'Bauls' (the crazy ones), itinerant beggars, singers, dancers and practitioners, who practice a secret, esoteric spiritual tradition, held within the guru-shishya (teacher-disciple) relationship. There are similar oral traditions in other parts of the country, such as in the Varkari tradition in Maharashtra or the Vachana tradition in Karnataka.

The three traditions have points of similarity as well as difference. All of them stress on the importance of a realized teacher (guru, murshid) and of a direct, unmediated learning experience in the body / self. In all of them, poetry and song become an intense medium of expression, communication and communion.

The tradition perpetuates itself in the form of a gathering: a 'satsang' (literally, gathering in and for truth), a 'jaagran' (all-night vigil), a Sufi 'sama' (musical gathering) or 'majlis' (assembly), or a Baul 'mela' (festival). People come together to sing and to listen, often at night, in the cool of the dark, free of other distractions, and also free of labour, as many of the people who participate work during the day at their trades, whether as artisans, farmers, cleaners, vendors or whatever else. The gathering may happen in the village square. It may happen in the courtyard of a temple or dargah. It may take place in a small room in someone's house. Or it may be just one itinerant fakir who starts to sing somewhere, whom people gather around to listen to.

There is singing—but not just songs. The singers are singing nothing less than truth itself. The listeners have a sense of participating in something important, which is not 'entertainment'. Several saint-poets rub shoulders with each other, as one song follows another. It is understood that 'all these people belong to the same tribe' (a phrase I have heard from several folk singers and lovers of poetry during my travels in Madhya Pradesh, Rajasthan and Gujarat). There is joy in speaking the same truth in the voice of a Kabir followed by the voice of a Meera or a Bulleshah. The sense of self expands as you participate in song and the spirit of truth, transcending for those moments all social limitations, restrictions and oppressions.

My mind has taken to fakiri
My heart has taken to living free
The joy that I find in meditation
Can't be found in luxury
—Kabir

Many of these seekers, practitioners, and singers have existed on the margins of society. Kabir and other 'Nirguni' poets (poets celebrating a formless divinity) are mostly preserved and sung by lower caste sections of society.* This is not without reason. Several of these poets themselves belonged to the lower castes. They rejected the upper caste stronghold on scripture, ritual and entry into temples. They pointed to a divinity within the temple of one's own body (thus the 'lower-caste', even 'untouchable', body was rendered divine). They attacked cant, hypocrisy, caste hierarchy, religious divisions, power structures, arrogance and foolishness. Those high up in the caste hierarchy or in religious power structures had no use for these poets. The saint-poets spoke with an authority based in their own experience (and not in scripture). And when the people who were socially marginalized began to sing them, they experienced this sense of power and authority in their own selves.

And yet the tradition is reverently irreverent. In spite of their savage critiques of social ills and corruptions, the saint-poets never lose hold of the dimension of a higher meaning, a 'truth' which they have experienced in their own bodies, and a sense of reverence for this higher reality. And thus the people who sing their songs after them, humble, everyday, ordinary people, derive also a strength which lies in having a vision, sense and purpose for their lives, which gives dignity, importance and centrality to their own bodies and selves.

Knowledge in the Body

This is perhaps the most critical element to be understood about the 'oral traditions' of 'mystic poets'. These songs speak of

*Sometimes this gets institutionalized as particular castes who practice an inherited music tradition as their vocation or profession, such as Meghwals, Mirasis, Langhas and Manganiars in Rajasthan.

knowledge in the body. This knowledge is communicated with the body through song. Therefore these songs—their singing and being heard—constitutes embodied knowledge.

Embodiment is a fundamental trait of this tradition. It is non-academic. It is not based around discourse or theorizing, but rather around song. The songs embody knowledge. The poets / singers / saints who originally composed or sang these songs were understood to embody knowledge. And the tradition insists that other singers who sing these songs must allow the knowledge coded or embodied in the song to inhabit their bodies in some way. It is common to come across statements such as these in the tradition: 'These are not just songs.' Or, 'You don't just sing this, as any other song.'

This sounds like a rather lofty idea, but at a practical level it is very close to the ground, and to the scores of humble farmers, fruit-sellers, labourers, sheep-rearers, weavers, leather workers, and other 'low caste' people who have kept these oral traditions alive through the act of singing—to them, the practice is immediate and evident.

In a broader sense the oral traditions allow a certain kind of looseness, the value of which we have forgotten in our ultra-exact, hyper-particular times. The same song may be ascribed in one context to Kabir and in another to Meera or Gorakhnath. It is not always clear how many of the songs ascribed to them were actually composed by them. Anyone—including you or I—has the freedom to compose a new song and add Kabir's name, for instance, to the signature line. Scores of such songs have been composed by seekers and practitioners and inhabitants of this land, and they have become part of the Kabir oral traditions.

This requires a different understanding of 'authenticity' or even authorship. Kabir, as mentioned before, never wrote. It took several decades before his songs began to be written down. There are disputes over the age of manuscripts and the authenticity of the songs written down in them; scholars have developed all kinds of apparatuses or systems to determine whether a song is an 'authentic' Kabir song or not.

In the oral tradition, the notion of authenticity is approached quite differently. Of course, there are endless distortions, corruptions and appropriations of the name of Kabir, for not always edifying purposes. There are all kinds of internal politics, carping, competition, jealousies, mutual disagreements and accusations, just like in any other field of activity. Having acknowledged this, I would like to focus on the strengths of this tradition, and how it offers us a whole new (or old) paradigm of understanding and knowledge, based in the subjective self, in the individual body.

It could broadly be asserted that the songs that take hold, get sung and repeated, become 'Kabir songs', even though they may have been composed much after Kabir's time. Of course, this is nowhere codified as such (in keeping with the tradition's overall non-codified spirit), yet this operates as a broad understanding. Bodies that sing, and listen, participate in creating the tradition. They act as a sieve. In this understanding, there is a sense of power or beauty that is associated with the epithet 'Kabir', and a song must live up to this promise. Those songs which do not may fall naturally by the wayside, without anyone having to explicitly expunge them. The tradition, in the long run, decides on the merits of each song. The tradition allows itself to make mistakes. And when I say 'the tradition', I mean the bodies that participate in the tradition through singing and listening. Given this large, loose, inclusive kind of spirit, the oral canon of Kabir songs is ever burgeoning. There is indeed no end to it.

We have several songs in the Kabir traditions which happily include anachronisms, such as guns, bullets, trains and so on. Even if everyone implicitly understands that this could not have been composed by Kabir in the fifteenth century, at the same time no one finds it necessary to assert that it is 'not a Kabir song' (except for scholars). On the contrary, it may be necessary to assert that it *is* a Kabir song.

Then there are songs in which Kabir and Gorakh, who lived at least four centuries apart from each other, are engaged in conversation. Followers of Gorakhnath will make Kabir acknowledge Gorakh to be his master in a song while followers of Kabir will do the reverse. It is futile to try to assert the primacy of historicity in this context because these conversations are understood to be at another plane altogether. At the same time no one necessarily believes that Kabir and Gorakh spoke physically with each other.

Apoorvanand, a well-known professor of Hindi literature at Delhi University, says in one place that, 'Kabir is a collective poetic voice that has evolved over centuries, one that the common folk of India have invented for themselves.'[1] The folk tradition honours the folk and their creative spirit. We must understand the tradition of Kabir (or of any other saint-poet) in this very broad sense.

The Subtle Fabric

This requires a certain amount of mental flexibility, and a peculiar faculty, or facility, which the modern, rationalist world seems to have deprived us of—namely, the understanding that a thing can be one thing, and not that thing, at the same time. In other words, it is not a question of binaries, of yes and no, of authentic versus inauthentic, of dogmatically declaring that, 'It is this and therefore it cannot be that'. A song can be a Kabir song and not a Kabir song at the same time. And no one needs to break their heads over it. Kabir himself says,

'Yes' doesn't quite catch it
'No' is not quite right
In the space between 'yes' and 'no'
My true guru hides

Why is this important, particularly for our age? It is important because it shows the ability to hold two (or more) truths in the mind at the same time. At a time of supposed globalization and hyper-communication, isn't it ironic that people seem to be getting more and more entrenched in their positions, their ideologies, their belief-systems? Is it contradictory to be scientific and to have faith at the same time? Must we align to the right or the left and find no space in between? Must categories be so hard and fast that they are always mutually exclusive?

As we entered the modern era, post-Renaissance through Enlightenment and the Industrial Revolution, we also entered the age of categories. A lot of modern knowledge is about categorizing, labelling, placing in the right order, and so on. This is a valuable enterprise, but to become slaves to only this way of thinking and knowing is tragic because it prevents a more supple, fluid and synthetic mind—one which is able to bring seemingly opposing categories or truths together in a higher understanding or truth.

The *Tao Te Ching* describes this trap of binaries, when it speaks consistently in terms of what we call 'paradox'. This is paradox only to a binary mind. To the more 'subtle perception', things are not so easily opposed.

If you want to shrink something,
you must first allow it to expand.

If you want to get rid of something,
you must first allow it to flourish.

If you want to take something,
you must first allow it to be given.

This is called the subtle perception
of the way things are.[2]

The Gurdjieff tradition* speaks of this reality in terms of 'three forces'—the affirming, the denying, and the reconciling. As long as we remain in the field of affirming versus denying, there is no real progress. It is only with the entry of the third force, the reconciling, that there is synthesis and evolution.[3]

Rumi describes the trap of binaries thus:

Out beyond ideas of wrongdoing and rightdoing,
there is a field. I'll meet you there.

When the soul lies down in that grass,
the world is too full to talk about.

Ideas, language, even the phrase: 'each other'
don't make any sense.[4]

The tradition speaks of this in terms of the three main energy channels described in Yogic terminology. These are ida-pingala-sushumna, often translated as left, right and central channels. 'Left' and 'right' is the field of duality—in-breath and out-breath, day and night, sun and moon, male and female, and so on. The poetry constantly urges us to move towards the 'central channel', one which is subtler than these divisions of yes-no, right-wrong, left-right, etc. This subtler truth is the gateway to a higher consciousness.

Ever since God became dead (according to the famous formulation of Nietzsche), there seems to be a discomfort in

*G.I. Gurdjieff was a twentieth-century Russian-Armenian teacher and mystic.

some circles with the notion of the 'higher'. While a distrust of hierarchy in the social sense makes perfect sense, and is indeed necessary in order to fight caste-, class- and gender-based discriminations which have persisted for centuries, this may be a misplaced enterprise in matters of the spirit. There is no meaning to the spiritual enterprise without a conception of the 'higher'. This poetry itself is nothing if it is not about the 'higher'. The mystic oral traditions themselves are meaningless if they do not deliver on their promise of a 'higher' or 'deeper' or 'subtler' (all these words denote the same thing) experience in the body.

The higher, or deeper, is what transcends dualities. It is the more subtle reality, hiding behind seeming differences and oppositions. The point is always to reach for the subtler and subtler truth. In the famous Kabir expression, this is called 'jheeni'. The cloth that he has woven with his poetry is subtle.

Woven from the fibre of Raam's name
This cloth is subtle, so subtle

The sound that he hears, that reverberates throughout the universe and also in his body, and which the oral traditions try constantly to recreate through song, singing and listening, is also 'jheena', or subtle.

In this sky, an instrument plays
Its sound is subtle, so subtle
—Kabir

Knowledge and Experience

The subtler is the higher or the deeper. It is not on the horizontal plane, where everything is flat and 'equal'. In the aphorisms of Sri Aurobindo, this is described as wisdom, as opposed to mere knowledge:

> Late, I learned that when reason died, then Wisdom was born; before that liberation, I had only knowledge.
>
> What men call knowledge, is the reasoned acceptance of false appearances. Wisdom looks behind the veil and sees.
>
> Reason divides, fixes details and contrasts them; wisdom unifies, marries contrasts in a single harmony.[5]

Sufi and Bhakti poets take endless and relentless digs at mere book knowledge, or any kind of learning which is not grounded in one's own experience—and experience is always in the body (which includes mind, whereas mind does not always include body).

Reading book after book
You've become a great scholar
But you never learnt to read yourself
—Bulleshah

You blabber fine words—do you live them?
What good is such wisdom, unlived?
Will it quench a thirsty heart's seeking?
Won't you wander again, lost, unhinged?
—Rohal Fakir

It's not a matter of reading and writing
It's a matter of experience!
When the bride and groom meet in union
The wedding party is of no significance
—Kabir

For these poets, mere conceptual knowledge is akin to being content to be in the wedding party—you may know all about union, you may discuss it endlessly, you may debate about it and develop wonderful theories, you may write papers and theses and books, you may expound on it till tears come to the eyes of your audience—but it is not the same as experiencing union.

And the experience of union, which is what these poets call 'prem' or 'ishq' or 'love', is subtle.

Reading all these dratted books
No one became wise
Read the four letters of love
That's how you become wise
—Kabir

Love as an abstract idea means very little. It has to be experienced in the body, between bodies. This tradition hinges on transmission—from body to body—much like love does. A sound is received as much in the body as it is by the mind (whereas text may be received only by the mind). Like love, which becomes real only when practiced, a song becomes itself only when sung and heard.

Word as Sound

Sound is subtler than text. Sound in the body is even more subtle than external sounds. And the subtlest sound of all is the 'anhad naad', that is, the 'unstruck sound', or the 'boundless sound', which is at once the sound in the individual body and the sound of the universe. This leap from the micro to the macro, and vice versa, is possible only because we are now in the realm of the subtle, where it is possible to pass from one element to another easily. At the level of the atom, outer differences vanish!

In this body, the sound of the universe
And fountains of elation, in this body
—Kabir

The Bhakti traditions featured in this book explicitly call themselves 'nirguni'. The 'sagun' form of Bhakti is devotion to a particular form of the divine, a specific deity. This could be Raam, Krishna, Shiva, Durga, Kali or any other form. This form is beheld with the eyes ('darshan'). The experience of the divine is visual. 'Nirgun' (literally, without attributes) Bhakti deals with reverence towards a formless divine, something which is beyond shape, form, qualities or attributes. It cannot be beheld with the eyes. Often, it is described in terms of sound ('naad'), sometimes light, at other times sky or space ('gagan'), and still others, 'shoonya' or emptiness. This fundamental, primordial sound, which cannot be heard with the ears, is also described as 'shabd', or Word.

This has obvious parallels in the Christian tradition and the idea of the 'Word of God':

> In the beginning was the Word, and the Word was with God, and the Word was God.[6]

A well-known song of Kabir, about listening to the subtle sound, says:

You came from Sound and Drop
And got formed in the waters here
It resides fully in everything
The invisible, unutterable Truth

The following verse from the Bible is very close to the way 'Word' is understood in the Bhakti oral traditions:

> For the word of God is alive and active. Sharper than any double-edged sword, it penetrates even to dividing soul and spirit, joints and marrow; it judges the thoughts and attitudes of the heart.[7]

But then the Word of God, in the Christian tradition, becomes text (or the book, that is, the Bible). In the Nirguni tradition, text is resisted, precisely because it becomes fixed. Sound is celebrated because it flows. Orality is the form of choice, because it cannot be pinned down. The idea of the 'original' and 'authentic' text does not carry so much favour. The idea of blasphemy cannot exist. The song exists in the moment, in someone's mouth, or throat. It is the truth of that moment. Someone may disagree with it (even vehemently) and sing it differently, or with the name of a different poet. Or the song may travel from one region to another, and adapt itself to the local tongue and flavour. In spite of this, there is an implicit trust, or pact, or contract, that the inner truth of the song is not disturbed by these outer, surface changes.

All this may sound like so much romantic nonsense to hardened, 'practical' ears. But we must not forget that while our current notions of practicality are only a couple of hundred years old, this tradition has survived, and thrived, much longer. It has done so because it has a basic confidence in itself. It does not consider the notion of 'inner truth' to be 'romantic', but to be a solid and indisputable fact. That it cannot be 'objectively verified' and put down in cold, hard black-and-white makes no difference to this tradition, because it does not believe in that paradigm anyway. These are popular modern notions of knowledge, influenced by the scientific paradigm. Of course, that paradigm has great value in its own place. But for the mystic tradition, truth is a deeply subjective experience, and yet universal at the same time. Again, the two are not opposed to each other.

Mystery and Mystification

The mystic tradition, consequently, is not afraid of mystery. If we were to think in a simplistic binary way, we would oppose the objectivity and factual emphasis of the post-Renaissance era to the mystifications and superstitions of the medieval era. But mystery and mystification are two different things. This poetry challenges the notion that everything there is to know can be known by the mind—but it does not say that everything cannot be known.

There are things which remain mysterious to the mind, but

are accessible to the spirit. The mystic does not say that these things cannot be known. On the contrary, she insists, even harps, on the fact, that this mystery needs to be penetrated and known, for oneself, by oneself, in oneself. Dominant modern paradigms of knowledge tend to resist the notion of phenomena which may lie outside the purview of the mind or of rational explanation. They posit an explainable universe.

The universe of the mystic is not flat. It is full of layers, of depths, of endless mysteries that unfold with great beauty. 'Who can speak about this?' they often ask. Or, 'This cannot be explained,' they often say. And yet poem after poem, song after song, speaks about precisely this. There comes with it a sense of wonder, exploration, discovery.

Therefore there is a basic comfort with the idea of mysticism. It is not viewed with suspicion. On the contrary, wonder in the face of mystery renders dumb the mind and its incessant chatter. The mystic sees the effects of the ordinary mind (disagreements, disputes, self-righteousness, judgement, wars), and therefore mistrusts it. The truth that she seeks has to be at a level higher than that of the ordinary mind.

And yet, Bhakti is no fuzzy or sentimental space, where one can comfortably float in a feel-good bubble. It is a place of sharp awareness. This faculty of awareness ('surat') is constantly distinguished from the mind ('mann'). The mind is the field of yes and no, right and wrong, us and them, full of thoughts and opinions, now blowing this way and now the other. Awareness is a subtler reality.

Who's the pot, who the churning stick
Who's the one who churns?
Mind, the pot, body, the churning stick
Awareness the one who churns

Let us examine what the Bhakti poets themselves say about Bhakti, starting with Kabir, who again points to the subtle truth which lies between dualities of either-or.

Seekers, the path of Bhakti is subtle!
Neither desire, nor lack of desire
Attention focused on surrender

A woman poet from Gujarat, Toral, is more explicit in the perilous and sharp nature of this path.

There is no measure of the Guru's greatness
Bhakti is like the tip of a sword

This is reminiscent of the Upanishads.

Get up! Wake up! Seek the guidance of an
Illumined teacher and realize the Self.
Sharp like a razor's edge, the sages say,
Is the path, difficult to traverse.[8]

Finally, Pritam Das, a poet from Sandesar village in central Gujarat, spells it out even better.

The path of Hari belongs to a warrior
Look, it's not for cowards, understand?
First of all, put down your head
Then think of walking, understand?

It may be useful to remind ourselves here that many of the poets in these traditions, as also the practitioners (singers, musicians, listeners) who have kept these traditions alive, have belonged to the marginal strata of society, primarily in terms of caste. They were acutely aware of the evils of mystification. Indeed, Kabir is well known for his trenchant critiques of the temple, the mosque, the idol, the call to prayer, fasts, observances, and all other manner of mechanical custom or ritual. And yet, this does not dissuade him from the realm of the mystical, the call of mystery. Perhaps this is the razor's edge that is invoked repeatedly—ruthless critique of what is false, and yet a deep reverence for the higher.

Spoken Truth

What if we tried to think about or understand the oral traditions of mystic poetry on their own terms?

The term used to describe this tradition of sung poetry is called 'vaani' or 'baani' (literally, voice or speech). A voice calling out, speaking to another, being heard, accepted and internalized, leading to another voice calling out. This is the 'vaani parampara', also called the 'shabd parampara' (voice or word tradition), which moves from body to body, and thus represents an embodied tradition (that is, not theorized and preserved in the abstract). This tradition needs voices. Voices need bodies. Bodies belong to people. Therefore, people own this tradition. They think of it as their own.

Recently I was in a small village called Chhella Karamashiya somewhere in central Gujarat. We were visiting an ashram maintained by Dalpatbhai Padhiyar, a seventh-generation singer of the vaani. He had invited several mandalis (literally, circles, but also used for musical or other kinds of groups) from surrounding villages for an evening and whole night of singing the vaani. One group of women from that village itself started up a bhajan. Dalpatbhai, sitting next to us, whispered in our ears: 'This is Kabir!' When the bhajan arrived near its conclusion, the women broke out into the last verse, bearing the signature of the poet. They sang it as a Gorakhnath bhajan. Immediately Dalpatbhai broke into a smile (instead of being racked by dismay), and spontaneously uttered into my ear: 'This is the miracle of the vaani. You can use anyone's signature. It will still be the truth.'

I was struck by the spontaneity of his response, as much as its content. In particular, I was struck by his use of one word: 'This is the *miracle* of the vaani.' Far from being embarrassed or apologetic about it, or even using a neutral word like 'characteristic' or 'quality', Dalpatbhai described it as nothing short of a miracle. What does this mean?

It is interesting to re-investigate notions of 'authenticity' and 'authority' in this light. The touchstone, or benchmark, applied by Dalpatbhai was equally striking—there is *truth*. It does not matter who said it, whether this poet or that one. Is there truth? If there is truth, then it is the vaani, whether you sing it as a Kabir or a Gorakhnath or a Bhavani Nath or Meera bhajan.* The notion of 'truth' applies as a benchmark because, as pointed out earlier, these are not mere poets—they are popularly held, regarded and revered as saints. They are 'saint-poets'. They utter poems or songs not for the sake being a poet, but because they must express the truth. A contemporary practitioner whom we have worked with closely, Parvathy Baul, describes the entire tradition as 'spoken truth'.

The benchmark for 'authenticity' is not whether this or that person spoke. The benchmark is: is it true? The benchmark for expertise or authority is not whether this person has this or that qualification or thesis or academic degree. It is quite simply: is the person widely held to be a saint? A saint is someone who has seen the truth and who therefore speaks the truth. Even more, he or she lives the truth. Of course, not all singers in the oral traditions have refined notions of truth or are above personal agendas. This is not even being claimed. Yet, the tradition insists that its touchstone is truth.

What, then, is 'truth'? For this tradition, in this tradition, and indeed for all Indian and perhaps even Eastern spirituality, it is

*I have personally seen interchanges in the signature lines of songs between all these poets.

the knowledge of the ultimate reality, the ultimate reasons and purposes behind existence. Anything expressing any fragment of this (and indeed, only fragments can be expressed) is the truth. This truth is not bolstered by 'theory'. It is curious that we seem to have arrived these days at the notion that knowledge can only be presented and understood in theories. Therefore, academic, scientific, economic and philosophic theories compete with each other. For the vaani tradition, because it deals with voice and expression and embodiment (the voice, unlike text, is in the body: this cannot be stressed enough), truth is always a matter of personal experience. And truth belongs to everybody—whoever chooses to embody it, in whatever way. It is neither the preserve of pundits with tomes of Sanskrit scripture nor of academics with sophisticated theories. Dalpatbhai said another striking thing in a completely sahaj (spontaneous, natural) way, which showed that it was embodied in him: 'Uska naam hi bhajan hai jo sab ka hai. (That which belongs to everybody, only that can be called a bhajan, or mystic song.)'

Song as Transformation

Thus we return to the notion of embodied knowledge. Embodied knowledge is, of necessity, different in different bodies—simply because each body is different from another. Just as the same song is sung differently by each singer, and yet all versions are 'true', the only condition being that they are sung with an inner authenticity. Thus, this notion of truth encompasses difference, and also oneness (again going beyond dualities). Only the truth can be universal, not knowledge, because it allows for difference.

This is an important distinction to make. The truth can be differently expressed at different places and times—just like a song—but it cannot be incorporated and frozen into any particular theory or structure. A theory may represent one dimension of knowledge, but it cannot claim to encapsulate truth. A song, precisely because it is momentary, never even makes this claim.

As I mentioned before, several of these poets existed outside the mainstream of society. Kabir (a weaver) and Ravidas (a leather-worker) belonged to the lower castes and were likely illiterate. The Nathpanthi saint-poets, such as Gorakhnath, Bananath, Bhavani Nath and others, belonged to an esoteric stream of spirituality, a yogic sect that kept itself outside the confines and rules of mainstream society. Meera could have been a queen but chose to leave the palace and to become a yogini. Shah Latif was a Sayyid, a descendant of the Prophet, but he chose to leave that high station and live like a fakir on top of a mound ('Bhit', therefore his honorific, 'Bhitai'). Bulleshah, too, was a Sayyid, born to a 'high caste', but he publicly forsook this station to become the disciple of a 'low caste' gardener. He further became the disciple of a 'dancing girl' (an even 'lower' station) in order to learn music and dance to please his master.

For all these people, on the margins of society, the notion of voice was extremely important. Their truths could only be voiced, on the margins, in a vulnerable and ephemeral form, needing to be ever recreated—in the shape of song.

One can't get it without singing
It's far from one who can't sing
Whoever sung it with confidence
Found the truth within
(Attributed to Kabir)

Anyone who has ever sung knows that song has the power to transform. A singer (or a dancer or any artist or seeker) is not the same person as when they are not singing. Singers we have interacted with say this and I can also vouch for it personally, having turned into a singer of this vaani myself. The person when she is singing is different from the same person when she is not singing. The song—especially these songs, because they are 'spoken truth'—hold power. At least momentarily, they can transform. This transformation can also be long-term. Songs themselves speak of this:

Gulabi Das sings, song transformed my body
It helped me overcome my flaws

The artist, in the moment of creating art, is 'inspired' (breathing in the divine). These songs go further. Because they are not merely art, but also truth, the singer in the moment of singing is touched by truth. He or she only has to become available to it. The song can touch the singer. Parvathy Baul says that the song even chooses the singer, and not the other way around. To be really touched is to become someone else.

To be transformed is the heart of the whole project. Not to know, but to be transformed. The songs are sung not only for their own sake, but also as vehicles for transformation. In the famous words of Kabir:

The redness of my beloved
Spreads in all directions
I set out in search of red
I became red myself!

Songlines Between Bhakti, Sufi and Baul

In the last few decades the idea of 'songlines' has come into the public imagination—singing the world into existence. The indigenous peoples of Australia believe in 'dreaming-tracks' made by creator spirits in 'dreamtime' (a time before or during creation), while they wandered over the continent. These tracks, which are also navigational aids and tools, are captured, preserved and passed on in stories and songs.

Borrowing this evocative idea, or at least the term 'songlines', we could say that the oral traditions of the subcontinent have traced these lines, in the bodies of various songs, dealing with common themes, ideas, symbols and concerns. This is what we have hoped to capture here.

It is an age-old and yet evermore pertinent question whether India has ever been a single nation. Is there anything that makes it one country, in spite of all its diverse languages, habits of dress and food, religions, sects, beliefs and practices?

In his wonderful Sahitya Akademi award-winning novel, *Tat Tvam Asi* ('You Are That'), the Gujarati writer Dhruv Bhatt describes 'adhyatma' (self-investigation or self-search), and an implicit or explicit knowledge or acknowledgement of the divine in the self, as the basis on which this civilization has survived, and rested, for centuries.

> All of us in this country are connected directly with 'Brahmn'. As I said before, all of us are children of freedom. This country has survived on spiritual knowledge, not religion… This country's mothers give the message of the Supreme Being to their children from their birth… The most ordinary illiterate person of this country also knows that he himself is a part of the Supreme Being.[9]

Looking at the oral traditions of Bhakti, Sufi and Baul mystic poetry in particular, we find that these distinct, unique and peculiar traditions share a commonality of concerns and themes. Together they present what has always been a hallmark of the Indic civilization—a celebration of diversity, with the underlying basis or understanding of oneness. They use similar metaphors, symbols and motifs to do so. They also critique, harangue, hit hard at precious beliefs, and encourage questioning and interrogation both of outer and inner beliefs. Some of the things they say are incredibly hard-hitting, particularly at the mores of the day.

They rip into religious and social orthodoxies which perpetuate exploitation and injustice. And yet, at the same time (not in opposition), they invoke a sense of the higher, a sense of the sacred.

This is the fundamental spirit and basis of this book. Across poets, across languages, across regions, across religions, the poets seem to address similar issues, utter similar cries, call out in similar ways, and express joy, loss, pain of separation, and the fulfilment of self-awareness, in similar ways. I have grouped these songs together along these lines. Hence, 'songlines'.

This book is a unique enterprise in that it seeks to bring together (to 'freeze' in print, if you like) songs which have hitherto largely flowed in the oral traditions. A few of these songs may never have been written down in textual compilations before. In any case, these traditions are now overflowing and spreading rapidly into urban areas. Modern methods of enregistering and fixing, such as audio and video recordings, are already a major factor in how the oral traditions are now talking to themselves. Singers share YouTube links and WhatsApp recordings with each other, and this is a new and faster way for exchanges within the tradition to grow. This book has two simple but fundamental purposes: to provide a glimpse of the songs of the oral traditions (as songs, and so we have retained refrains for many of the poems here), and to trace and emphasize a commonality of spirit and inquiry between the Bhakti, Sufi and Baul traditions.

The songlines presented here trace out different paths for the seeker to traverse. These lines were perhaps traced originally in 'dreamtime', and the poets have only given words in different ways to maps that have always been in our consciousness. Be that as it may, here is one possible map.

These songs could have been arranged in different ways without much trouble. A single song speaks of multiple themes. However, in this moment, for this book, I found it useful and meaningful to arrange them in this way. In the spirit of the oral traditions, I would not claim this to be the 'best' arrangement, either of the sections or of the songs within them. This is merely the truth of the moment. Each song can be 'best' only in the moment in which it is being sung.

These songs have travelled all over the country. They have perhaps seen more of our country than many of us living here. They have lived in various bodies, inhabited many throats, spoken in several languages and dialects. Perhaps they are more alive than most of us living today or yesterday. They have certainly lived longer. They show a striking kinship to each other across Bhakti, Sufi and Baul traditions, pointing to a common bloodstream running through these various bodies of poetry and song. They embody a core spirit that runs through the veins of the whole of Indic civilization, from scriptures to all its arts and crafts—a living relationship with the sacred.

And yet, these songs find voice in the bodies of ordinary people such as weavers, farmers, sweepers, artisans and so on, who sing in the ordinary register of speech which belongs to the people, and not in any 'high' erudite or philosophic verse. This is why these lines of song have travelled so widely and stayed alive for so long.

A Thousand Doorways

The songs presented here are a selection from the thousands of songs which flow like rivers through this land. The same song will often be found in different regions with slight variations of text, often in different tunes. We have chosen the versions that we got connected with personally.

This includes the words in a particular version as well as the poet it is ascribed to (as the same song may well be ascribed to another poet in another area or version). So the name of the poet and the region mentioned below each song belong to the particular version that we have chosen. It does not mean that the song originally comes from Rajasthan or Malwa, or belongs only to Rajasthan or to Malwa. It simply means that the version translated here is what we heard in Rajasthan or Malwa or Kutch or Sindh or wherever.

It is important to remember not to take any of the songs here as 'definitive' texts in any sense. They are presented here in the spirit in which they flow in the oral traditions—loose, joyful, playful, alive. Some songs may have been sung only partially when we heard them, and I have not always bothered to 'complete' them (sometimes I have). Some songs are mixed up with verses which might belong to other poets or other songs, and I have not always bothered to 'correct' them. We have translated the song as it came alive for us at a particular moment.

For instance, the song translated here as 'Leave Your Charades, O Yogi' (p. 48) is usually attributed to Kabir. But the version which we heard in the powerful voice of Jamali Bai of Bikaner had Gulabi Das as the poet. So we have mentioned the poet as Gulabi Das, not Kabir. As I said, the poet and region mentioned under each song are not definitive in any sense.

Or, the song translated here as 'In This Body' (p. 168) is sung slightly differently in Malwa. In Malwa it is a longer song, and has a totally different emphasis in the refrain from the evocative refrain chosen here ('But you search in the dark!'). The refrain in the Malwa version is longer and translates something like:

Only one who can know will know
Without the guru, the world is dark

This is a totally different emphasis from the version that we have chosen, which we have heard in several urban singers' voices, and which has a much more mocking quality to it (the light is within you, yet you insist on searching in the darkness!).

There are many more such examples. Linda Hess, a well-known scholar of Kabir from Stanford University, has written extensively about this fluidity and flexibility of the oral traditions in her book *Bodies of Song*.[10]

Contemporary poets have also happily walked into this mix, because this tradition just does not deal in hard-and-fast categories. So we have songs by Madan Gopal Singh, Parvathy Baul and Dhruv Bhatt, contemporary poets and / or singers and practitioners, rubbing shoulders with Kabir, Gorakh, Meera and others, although the collection is largely comprised of the poets flowing in the oral traditions for several centuries. Apart from the very well-known Bhakti poets, such as the ones mentioned above, or others from the Sufi and Baul traditions such as Bulleshah, Shah Latif or Lalon Fakir, there are also several poets about whom we know literally nothing other than their name appearing in the signature line of a song. They also find their place easily in this pantheon of poets, because their songs have become part of the stream of tradition of song—fluidity and flow being one of its defining characteristics. As I have tried to express throughout this introduction, this outer flexibility is based on an inner conviction of unity and truth, and this I take to be a hallmark of Indic life and civilization. The usual example cited in this regard is quite germane and I will take this opportunity to cite it again: the proliferation of endless gods and sects and even versions of the same sacred text (eg. the Ramayana or the Mahabharata) in what we today call 'Hinduism', speaks of this quality. Though this flexibility and largeness of spirit, which allows for multiple forms and expressions, is under threat today, it does remain a deep well which will hopefully outlast this current narrowness of outlook and continue to nourish our spirit.

Note on Translations

The translations in this book have evolved over the period of a considerable number of years. The extraordinary work started by

Shabnam as the 'Kabir Project' in 2002, which I had the good fortune to join at a later date, has led us into a long-term and intensive engagement with the oral traditions of these songs as they are sung and interpreted in different parts of our land.

Consequently, a lot of our focus has been on maintaining an approach that balances the viewpoint of these traditions towards these songs together with the literary considerations of translation into English. Our effort is consistently to translate the spirit of these songs, as we understand them, which is heavily influenced by our interactions with and learnings from the practitioners of these songs from different traditions. Foremost among them are Prahlad Tipanya and Kaluram Bamaniya from Malwa, Mahesha Ram from Jaisalmer, Parvathy Baul from Bengal / Trivandrum, the late Abdullah Hussain Turk from Kutch, among many others. They have shaped our absorption of the spirit of these songs.

Shabnam and I have worked together over several years to translate these and other songs, so much so that at some point, in several cases, it is impossible to distinguish one's contribution from the other's. A lot of the translations are done together and are credited as such, but a great number of songs have also been translated individually, with inputs from the other. The appropriate credits for each individual translation in the section designated for this can be found at the back of the book.

A Wondrous City

I will not speak too much about the limitations and challenges of translation. Almost every translator in every book of translation addresses this question. I would rather speak of the joys of translation. While translating certain terms, expressions, idioms, especially from this kind of poetry, is highly difficult, if not impossible, there is also the joy of creating something new altogether, a fresh understanding (for ourselves), in a different language. Sometimes when Shabnam and I read each other's, or others', translations, without knowing the original, we think, 'Wow! What song is this?' This is because often a translation can lead to an entirely new way of looking even at something which was known intimately in the original language. Apart from staying very close to the original, this recreation of spirit has been our brief—to reinterpret the song afresh from our own understanding.

Our work at the Kabir Project over several years has led us from one song to another, one poet to another, with always a sense of fresh discovery. Like an ocean, these traditions are fathomless. There is always a fresh new song, or a fresh new voice, to stumble upon, with delight and joy. These traditions are very much alive today, these streams have started flooding even the cities now, and everyone who hears or sings these songs helps in keeping them alive and participates in the tradition.

We invite you to experience these verses also as songs, on the digital platform or web archive that we have been constructing for almost a decade now as part of our work at the Kabir Project, located within Srishti Institute of Art, Design and Technology in Bengaluru. The archive is called 'Ajab Shahar' (www.ajabshahar.com), that is, a 'wondrous city', a reference to the cities that are our own bodies, a metaphor used by several songs in the tradition. Wandering through this digital city you may come across different versions of the same song, with different words or tune or singer, or maybe all three. You might also find multiple translations for the same song. You might lose yourself entirely, only in order to find yourself again. This book, here, now, is presented to you as a small drop from the vast ocean of the vaani. And yet, as Kabir says, the drop contains the whole ocean.

Drop in the ocean
Everyone knows
Ocean in the drop
A rare one knows

So, taking a cue from our first song, one could set out from one's house, after setting it ablaze and gutting it thoroughly, place one's feet on the path, toughen up in one's practice, confront suffering, loneliness and the pain of longing, and then one might arrive at the moment of immersing in the ocean, and learn the art of dying, in order to arrive eventually in the beloved's country and experience fulfilment. One might then experience an immersion in the river of love, with which this book ends. Do travel along the lines of these themes, as arranged in the book—or along any other lines of your own that you choose to make up. The journey is your own.

VIPUL RIKHI

Goa,

June 2019

1. GHAR / HOUSE

What is it about a house that makes us feel secure? The four walls. The roof above the head. The warmth, comfort, feeling of home. Perhaps other people. Relationships. Food, nurture, rest. All this is connected with the feeling of 'house'.

But what if the walls that protect are also walls that imprison? And what if the roof that shelters us is also the limit that makes us small? And what if the comfort that we cherish is also what keeps us narrow?

These are difficult questions. But no one said that the mystic experience or quest was an easy one. Those who promise only 'elevating' experiences in the name of spirituality or mysticism probably mislead. True mystics promise only a trial by fire. A path of suffering. A long quest. Cutting off the head. Burning down one's house.

Kabir stands in the marketplace
Flaming torch in hand
Those who can burn their house
Come, walk with me

Walking with Kabir is no easy task, no stroll in the park. One has to burn one's house down. What are the houses we live in? There is, of course, the physical house, which often takes many years or a whole lifetime to build. One works for it, one carefully constructs it, one decorates it lovingly. This is the same that we do for our self-image—worked at diligently, carefully constructed, lovingly decorated. And what a flare-up there is when somebody, especially a near and dear one, threatens this painstakingly built-up structure! Is this not another house that we live in?

Then there are the ideas or ideologies that one holds very dearly. We are ready to fight, struggle, kill or die for these ideas or beliefs. Are they not another house? And then there are the emotions that we revel in. These could be centred around self-congratulation or self-pity (or both), around self-righteousness or a feeling of victimhood. Do they not constitute another house that we inhabit?

And are these houses not very fragile, constantly buffeted by external storms and winds? And are we really secure in these houses, or do we feel anxious and worried about losing them?

How many such houses have we built up around us? In how many mansions do we move? How much burning down will we have to do? How many flaming torches?

In his moment of awakening, the Buddha is reputed to have said: 'Housemaker, you are seen. Now you shall not build any more houses!' And in the Buddhist tradition, those who renounce samsara (externally or internally) are called the 'left-home ones'.

Kabir says, 'I make my house on the tip of a thorn / That's where I'm most at ease.' What is this if not comfort with not making oneself comfortable, a razor-sharp and constant alertness?

Kabir has other ways to describe a larger sense of house too.

I plunged into the ocean
And emerged in the sky!
I built my house in the sky-circle
And found many jewels there

He also describes the 'house of love' as a very tough place indeed.

This is the house of love
Not your favourite aunt's place!

Cut off your head, put it on the floor
Then think of entering

In the Sufi tradition, Rahib evokes the highest station as that of 'being without a house' or without a point (la-makaan). One who is not fixed or located. Un-pin-down-able. An attribute of god.

An unknown fakir from Bangladesh writes a Baul song in the voice of Radha, who cries:

Kaala, my dark beloved
Has driven me crazy
How can I stay at home?

For a woman, traditionally, the ultimate transgression is to leave the home and its confines, where her (and her family's) honour and pride are secure. The call of Krishna makes women leave their homes, their families, their children, their 'honour', and everything else that they are instructed to uphold. Leaving home can be a radical act.

If we would embrace the wide universe, we must step out of our house. And then, in a curious reversal, sometimes the universe comes to abide in the house. Which house? Perhaps the house of the body, this self. Many Sufi songs repeat this trope, like this famous one by Amir Khusro:

O friend, my lord has come home
My courtyard has been blessed

The guru, or the beloved, or this wisdom, comes home at last ('Mera piya ghar aaya'). That's when this house finally becomes a habitation fit to dwell in.

What are the contours of 'my house'? How narrow or broad are the rooms? How much light or air is let in? Is it cluttered with things and knick-knacks or does it embody a sense of space? This poetry invites us to examine our relationship to our own houses—

the physical ones and the ones in the mind and heart. How tightly do we cling to them? How much would we engage in battle for them? And how willing, or unwilling, are we to abide in a vaster, freer space?

The Drink of Raam

I burnt down my house, yogi
I took up the flaming torch
If you scorch your own house, yogi
Then join me on this walk

The drink of Raam is incredibly sweet
One who drinks it never dies

Scorch the house to make a house arise, yogi
Protect it and it's gone!
I saw a miraculous sight, yogi
A dead man eating up time
The drink of Raam…

A fire blazes ahead, yogi
In its wake, greenery thrives
I'm devoted to that tree, yogi
Cut the root and the fruit revives
The drink of Raam…

Dhruv drank it, Prahlad drank it, yogi
Peepa and Ravidas drank it in
Kabir too is drinking, yogi
Thirsty to drink it again and again
The drink of Raam…

—Kabir; Rajasthan

Kaala, My Dark Beloved

Kaala, my dark beloved
Has driven me crazy
How can I stay at home?

Kaala! O, Kaala!
My heart calls out, friends
He is my necklace
The golden form
Etched in my heart
How can I stay at home?

Kaala! O, Kaala!
I call out, friends
He's my garland
A flame that flickers within
Kaala is life and death itself
How can I stay at home?

I went to the banks
Of song and sound
I glimpsed his form
Reflected in the waters
Don't stray that way alone, friend
You might end up like me
How can I stay at home?

*

I can't hold onto
Honour and pride anymore

What should I do? Where can I go?
I can't see the way ahead
Honour and pride slip away…

What sort of love is this?
It makes me snap all my ties
Honour and pride slip away…

My heart smoulders
Like fire in paddy husk
Slowly, incessantly
Honour and pride slip away…

Who can know my plight?
My heart is not
In this world any more
Honour and pride slip away…

O listen, friend!
Who can know my yearning
In this deluded world?
Honour and pride slip away…

I'm steeped in love
For Kaala, my dark beloved
My life is wrecked
Honour and pride slip away…

Listen to my sorrow, friend
Kaala, my dark beloved
Has driven me crazy
How can I stay at home?

—Unknown;* Bengal

*This song is ascribed by Parvathy Baul to an unknown fakir from Bangladesh. Apparently, it is based on the last few moments of Radha's life, just before she walks into the Yamuna river mistaking it to be Krishna. Both the Yamuna and Krishna are black in colour: 'kaala' means black.

One Without a House

In every particle you dwell
O one without a house!
You inhabit all spaces
O one without a house!

I set out and saw the earth
I saw the lord there
On earth I came across Adam
Adam's breath is you
O one without a house!

I set out and saw the sky
I saw the lord there
In the sky I encountered stars
The moon among them is you
O one without a house!

I set out and saw the mosque
I saw the lord there
In the mosque I saw the mihrab
The mihrab points to you
O one without a house!

I set out and saw the temple
I saw the lord there
In the temple I saw an idol
The idol's spirit is you
O one without a house!

I set out and saw the ocean
I saw the lord there
The ocean has endless waves
The jewel in the depths is you
O one without a house!

I set out and saw the boat
I saw the lord there
I met Rahib, the boatman
Rahib's navigator is you
O one without a house!

—Rahib; Kutch

The Lord Has Come Home

The lord has come home today
Bliss and joy pour down in my heart

O yes, the banks of the river are steep
While the water is lying low
I climbed to the top and met my guru
He dwells where the three rivers flow
The lord has come home today…

O yes, I sprinkle saffron dust
And deck his seat with silk
And yes, I scent it with sandalwood
And wash his feet with milk
The lord has come home today…

O yes, I plant a cardamom tree
An evergreen creeper shoots out
And yes, I fashion a crown of flowers
In the heart's soil, the buds sprout
The lord has come home today…

O yes, I looked far and wide for Hari
I found him all too near
And yes, the seeker was set free
Open your eyes, Kabir
The lord has come home today…

—Kabir; Rajasthan

My Girlhood Home

I have no joy in my parents' home anymore
My old home, my girlhood home

The beloved's city
Is of breath-taking beauty
Where no one enters or leaves
No sun or moon
No wind or water
Who can take my message there?
Who will tell him of my pain?
I have no joy...

I can't find the way ahead
To turn back would be folly
How can I reach
The beloved's house, O friend?
The fever of longing burns me
Sensual delights make me
Dance to their tune
I have no joy...

Who can you call your own
Except the true guru
Who else can show the way?
Kabir says, listen seekers
The beloved doesn't come in a dream
To douse the heart's flames
I have no joy...

—Kabir; Malwa

The House of Love

This is the house of love
Not your favourite aunt's place!
Cut off your head, put it on the floor
Then think of entering

*

Kabir's house is on a peak
And the path there is tricky
Even an ant's foot slips there!
O mind, why load your bullock-cart?

*

I plunged into the ocean
And emerged in the sky!
I built my house in the sky-circle
And found many jewels there

*

Beyond the elements and the energies
Lies the abode of freedom
Kabir makes his home where there's no one
No Gorakh, nor Dutt, nor Raam…

—Kabir; Malwa (set of couplets)

2. SONGS OF THE PATH

'Song' and 'road' have always evoked each other. Whenever we set out, we carry our music with us, either in technological devices or in our hearts and tongues. So if we are on the road, a song arises. If a song arises in the stillness of our homes, it can feel like we are being 'transported'. It's not surprising then that there are many songs *of* the road itself, songs of the path.

The poets call out to us as musaafir (traveller), pardesi (foreigner), doora desi (traveller from distant lands), panchhi (bird), hansa (swan), bhanwara (bee), banjaara (nomad or gypsy) implying a journey, a flight, a search, a wandering…

Come, come, whoever you are
Wanderer, worshipper, lover of leaving
It doesn't matter
Ours is not a caravan of despair
Come, even if you've broken your vow
A thousand times
Come, yet again, come, come
—Rumi[11]

Sometimes it's an intimate and compelling call to 'take to the road', and sometimes it is a scolding tone shaking us out of the inertia of 'being stuck'. The poem hits us on the head with a sense of urgency.

He's not found
By sitting on your ass
He's not found
On a soft, warm bed
He's found by those
Who walk the path
And weep for him
—Shah Latif

Then again the invitation could be seductive, cajoling us to another land, another country, a doorway to another way of being?

Let's go, my sweet
To the guru's country
Where nothing arises
And nothing subsides
—Kabir

This particular journey—the one to self-awareness—is long, arduous and rough. The songs offer encouragement, faith and hope, or caution us about the pitfalls that await on the path.

Travel light, the poets say. How will you walk this path with so much baggage: material, emotional, ideological?

Leaving all your clothes behind
Set out stark naked
Those who walk with nothing
Reach farthest
—Shah Latif

Metaphors of the vehicle abound. The body-self is a train, a horse-carriage or a bullock-cart, tottering down the path of life, getting mired in the mud or worn down by the fast pace. Sometimes it's a boat tackling the waves of the bhavsaagar, the ocean of becoming.

Some songs describe a yogic pathway, in which our life-force or kundalini makes the tough upward journey through the central energy channel piercing through the chakras to the crown of the head. A journey of but a few feet—from the bottom of the torso to the top of the head—but one that may well take a lifetime to traverse!

In one sense, we walk a path where a thousand have walked before us, spinning in the same cycles of confusion and often despair. Lost and utterly absorbed as we are in our personal narratives, which seem so important and unique, these songs give us a bird's-eye view of a reality we miss: *Sab chala chali ka khela!* (It's all a game of come-and-go!)

At the end of our journey, we might discover that we needn't have walked so far or struggled so much. And yet, how could we know this without having walked so far or struggling so much? These poems seem to call for both movement and stillness, perhaps a movement towards stillness.

You run and you run
As far as your mind can run
When it tires, the mind halts
You are at your destination
—Kabir

We shall not cease from exploration
And the end of all our exploring
Will be to arrive where we started
And know the place for the first time
—T.S. Eliot, 'Little Gidding'

There is another journey—one that implies a parting, a farewell, a letting go—which we don't wish to undertake and which we resist bitterly. It is the final journey, and the one who comes to take us on it is the batavado, literally 'the one of the road'. As the song of the batavado unfolds, we realize with a shock that this groom who has come to fetch his bride is, in the imagination of Kabir, a metaphor for death itself.

You've Been Walking for Ages

O Kabir
You've been walking for ages
Who will show you the way?
Without insight, the mind wanders
Home is just a step away

O Kabir
Who's the pot, who the churning stick
Who's the one who churns?
Mind, the pot; body, the churning stick;
Awareness the one who churns

O Kabir
Kabir, the seeker, drank the ghee
The world's content with buttermilk
Why worry if you drank the ghee?
The cow is with the creator
Feed her the fodder of your love
You'll get her milk forever

O Kabir
The arrow of attention darts everywhere
Hold it still if you can
The warrior stays in the battlefield
The coward runs for cover

O Kabir
I make my house on the tip of a thorn
That's where I'm most at ease
Wise Kabir is absorbed in play
Alert each moment of night and day

—Kabir; Rajasthan

If You Really Want

If you really want to get across
Prepare right away!
Give all you have to the guru
Do it cheerfully, seeker
But if your mind refuses to submit
No point blaming the guru, seeker!

Once the mind's been persuaded
Don't pull back or hesitate
The guru's the manifest giver of freedom
Dwell within her gaze
Do it cheerfully, seeker

Three lines of energy in the body
Make your home in the central string
Adopt the inward-looking position
Chant the nameless chant of remembering
Do it cheerfully, seeker

See how in and out breaths get created
Stay absorbed in that vision
Daduram says, in the guru's refuge
The self finds liberation
Do it cheerfully, seeker

—Daduram; Malwa

Climb Slowly, My Friend

Climb slowly, my friend, O swan
Climb carefully, dear brother!

A hundred miles and countless leagues
And no trail safely winding up
An ant can't keep its footing here, swan
How will you go climbing up?
Climb carefully…

On the way your new-wed awareness
Sings the song of detachment
Don't drown in the ocean of becoming, swan
Don't immerse in attachment
Climb carefully…

The path is narrow, the way is harsh
Steep and rough the incline
Lasso the breath and make it mount, swan
In the central channel of the spine
Climb carefully…

I've found Ramanand, my true guru
He's told me the secret sign
Kabir says, O swan, the cycle
Of come-and-go has been left behind
Climb carefully…

—Kabir; Malwa

The Cart of Meditation Is Tottering

Your meditation-cart is tottering
Remember the creator, O heart
Who blocks your path?

Wood from five forests
From ten forests, the pegs
Nine months to fabricate
For a thousand miles it rolls its legs
The cart of meditation…

The camel who pulls it is a fool
Yoke it with the reins of truth
Load it with freight of the Name
The guru's words chart out the route
The cart of meditation…

Your wife is by your side with food
Served on love's eastern plate
Gulp it down remembering Hari
Go on, I'm behind you, he says!
The cart of meditation…

Raam's name, the wares you cart
The eternal Name, your wages
Fakru says thus you will remove
Your knots of endless ages
The cart of meditation…

—Fakru; Rajasthan

Drive This Cart Slowly

Drive this cart slowly
O my Raam of this cart
Drive this cart gently
O my Raam of this cart

This cart is colourful, beautiful
The wheels are red and rosy
A sassy young girl holds the reins
Raam sits in the vehicle
Drive slowly…

The cart got stuck in the sand
And the destination is far away
The true ones made it there
The criminals got crushed
Drive slowly…

Healers from many lands were called
They brought their herbs and cures
None of this was of any use to you
When your link to Raam got broken
Drive slowly…

Four people lift the stretcher
And prepare a wooden carriage
Drive to the funeral grounds
And up it goes in flames like Holi
Drive slowly…

The woman weeps in great distress
Our couple has been torn apart
Kabir says, listen seekers
The one who unites, separates
Drive slowly…

—Kabir; Malwa

It's All a Game of Come-and-Go

It's all a game of come-and-go
Our meetings in this world are fleeting
It's all a game of come-and-go

Someone's going, someone's gone
Someone's packing their bags to go
Someone stands alone, ready for the road
It's all a game of come-and-go

Mother, father, siblings and friends
No one comes along at the end
Why fill your bag with sins and woes?
It's all a game of come-and-go

Plotting and scheming in the web of life
You amassed a million in wealth
Couldn't take a penny when you went
It's all a game of come-and-go

The world's in the throes of death
Meditate on the master, my friend
Brahmanand says, listen seeker
It's all a game of come-and-go

—Brahmanand; Kutch

O My Heart, Let's Go Home

O my heart, let's go home
This world is a foreign land
Why do you wander here
In a stranger's clothes?

These desires and earthly loves
Are alien, not your own
Infatuated with strangers
You forget the one, your very own
O my heart, let's go home…

Climb the path of truth, O heart
Light a lamp of love to show the way
Take the wealth of virtue along
Guard this treasure well
O my heart, let's go home…

Gathering of true seekers
Are resting places on this road
If you fall in doubt, ask the way
From one who walks this road
O my heart, let's go home…

The bandits of greed and delusion
Lie in wait to loot you on this path
Fend them off with the guards
Of stillness and restraint
O my heart, let's go home…

If you see scary shapes and forms
Take the name of that powerful king
The one who rules this road
Even Death bows down to him
O my heart, let's go home…

—Ajoyoddyanath Pakrashi; Bengal

No Time for Loitering

He's not found by sitting on your ass
He's not found on a soft, warm bed
He's found by those
Who walk on the path and weep for him

If you wish to die tomorrow
The beloved will come tomorrow
Or never at all
It has never been
That one living in comfort
Found him

Don't wail without a true cry
Don't walk without a true gait
Don't burn without true fire
Don't weep without true tears

Burn as long as you live, Sasui!*
There is no rest without burning
In heat and cold, keep walking
This is no time for loitering

—Shah Latif; Kutch (set of couplets)

Sweetheart, Dear Girl

Sweetheart, dear girl
Wake up your beloved
He sleeps a deep, forgetful sleep
Shake him awake!

On the banks of the navel-lotus
A female serpent sways
Five thieves stick close to her
Her life-force fades
Sweetheart, dear girl…

Within the heart-lotus
Awareness is aroused
She takes on four lovers
Her life-force awakens
Sweetheart, dear girl…

---

*For a brief exposition of the story of Sasui and Punhu, see the chapter introduction to the section 'The Truth of Suffering'.

In a whirling cave
The buzzing of a bee
It drinks in a subtle fragrance
Now it cannot sleep
Sweetheart, dear girl…

My eyes have become rapt
Open your eyes too, my love
In a flash, my sleep is gone
Awake, speak a few pleasant words
Sweetheart, dear girl…

Kabir says, think about this
A rare one awakens
She who comes to the guru's door
All illusions dispelled
Sweetheart, dear girl…

—Kabir; Kutch, Rajasthan, Cholistan

The Traveller's Come to Take Me Away

The traveller has come
To take me away
Save me just this time, oh mother!
Your son-in-law has come
To take me away!

Eight rooms and ten doors
In this body-temple of mine
I scramble and run from one to another
My dratted foe won't let me hide!
O, the traveller has come…

With due respect, the traveller said
Listen, old mother, to what I say
I've got orders from Raam himself
I arrived in the dead of the night
Your son-in-law has come…

The old woman made a humble plea
Listen, oh guest, to what I say
My daughter is out with friends
She's just at an age to play!
O, the traveller has come…

Monsoon days have just begun
The festival of Teej is here
My girl's so young and innocent
Let her go just this once!
Your son-in-law has come…

Seven friends gathered around
Plaited her hair in braids
Now she's ready, the mother said
Give her some good advice!
O, the traveller has come…

Five brothers of the darling girl
Came to bless their sister
Family and clan were left behind
She took this road alone
Your son-in-law has come…

Says Kabir, listen oh seekers
See the point of what I say
This marital home will claim us all
Meditate on this well
O, the traveller has come…

—Kabir; Malwa & Rajasthan

3. TOUGHEN UP

What might be the difference between being 'moved' and being 'wounded'? The experience of being moved lasts perhaps a few hours or a few days. The experience of being wounded cuts deeper. It burns into the fabric of your being and lingers in the memory of your body. It changes you forever.

Kabir often speaks of a 'shabd ki chot' (wound from the Word) or 'aasmaan ki chot' (wound from the sky).

What do you know of the pain of others?
If you were struck by the Word, you'd know
If you were wounded by Song, you'd know

*

I'll strike home, seeker!
This wound is from the sky

Being 'moved' comes cheap in our globalized, media-saturated times. As consumers of a thousand expressions, ideas and events pouring into our lives through digital screens, we are 'touched' by many things, but transformed by nothing. We profess to feel deep emotions which are immediately translated into social media posts. Our experiences of beauty or love seem to be merely verbal, and more for show, rather than with any real depth of feeling. How could it be otherwise, in the pace of life we now inhabit? Where is the time or space to experience anything, much less a wound?

This poetry gives a right kick in the balls to any tepid, feel-good notions of bhakti or devotion, which are devoid of a tough, even painful, self-interrogation. The spiritual path is not a way to feel good about oneself, to imagine extraordinary meditational experiences, or to eulogize miracle-working gurus, or to pursue the same ambitions or need to be special that we bring to worldly concerns. The path is difficult because it will destroy our delusions about ourselves. It will humble us in the true sense of the word. It is not for every fool to buy a ticket and walk in.

My guru's out on a hunt
Red bow in hand
The fools escaped unscathed
The true seeker got struck down

*

The whole world is happy
It eats and sleeps
Kabir alone is miserable
He wakes and weeps

Why is the encounter with the guru described as a wound? Is it because this wisdom doesn't come easy? Because it requires a transformation we have been resisting?

Many of us are susceptible to this curious paradox—we are all for transformation, as long as we don't have to change! We resist having to confront our self-indulgent habits, or our delusional self-images. We harbour cotton-headed ideas about the 'Sufi' path or the way of 'surrender'. We even imagine we are on the path, without actually giving up anything.

It is in this backdrop of feeling-good that this poetry reminds us that there is nothing much to feel good about in our current situation. As the first song in the section says: devotion's tough, my friend! The path of love for the guru, or this wisdom, is hard.

One has to stay the course when the going gets tough. One has to work with a will. One has to suffer many blows. One has to 'walk the talk'. Above all, one has to 'shed personal wants and cares'. The pot has to be baked fully in fire and heat. These are tough prescriptions.

Will you ever become a Baul with your half-baked efforts? asks a Baul song sarcastically. *If you want to enter the house of love, cut off your head and put it on the floor,* says Kabir. Shah Latif asks the crow to pluck out his eyes if they do not behold the beloved at the break of dawn.

The last song in this section speaks of the story of Beejal and Rai Diach, as interpreted by Shah Latif. Beejal, a wandering minstrel, plays music outside the palace of King Rai Diach of Junagadh, moving him beyond words. Wounding him, perhaps. The king summons Beejal to his court and commands him to name his price for playing such divine music. Beejal, to the surprise of the whole court, including the king, asks for the king's head. Rai Diach, a man of his word, complies. Mourning descends on Junagadh, but Rai Diach himself could not be happier.

Latif uses this story as a spiritual metaphor. The minstrel, the beggar, is the guru, who asks for the head, the ego-self. The king is the willing seeker, ready to pay the price. Music is the overarching figure for this transformation. Will it take anything less than this, Latif seems to ask.

For those of us harbouring fluffy, romantic ideas about the 'spiritual path', this poetry comes as a rude wake-up call. It's a game of death. Everything's at stake—to be won, to be lost.

Devotion's Tough, My Friend!

Devotion's tough, my friend!
Love for the guru is hard
Without it, acts have no grace
You swim to your apocalypse

Like the brainfever bird calls crazily
For rain under an auspicious star*
It prefers death in longing
To any other water at any other hour
Devotion's tough...

Like armies ranged against each other
Brave warriors take up the fight
They get hacked and slashed to pieces
But never dream of resorting to flight
Devotion's tough...

Like the deer drawn to the Word
It knows the secret of sound
It gives up its life to hear the Word
Not a shred of fear to be found
Devotion's tough...

Shedding personal wants and cares
Sing of greatness fearlessly
When, says Kabir, such is your devotion
The guru will appear spontaneously
Devotion's tough...

—Kabir; Malwa

---

*Legend holds that the rain which falls under the Swati Nakshatra (the fifteenth house of the moon in the Indian system of astrology) is so auspicious / powerful that it causes pearls to form in shells, and the 'chaatak', a legendary bird, here called 'papeeha' (the hawk-cuckoo or brainfever bird), drinks only of this rain.

Love-Water Does Not Stay

Love-water does not stay, dear one
In a half-baked pot
In an unbaked pot

The clay of an unbaked pot
Will crumble in the water
Then you'll find yourself
In a fine soup!
Love-water does not stay…

If you would only bake your pot
You'd arrive at the guru's house
Polished there in the traits of love
You would sparkle with beauty
Love-water does not stay…

Sadanand Goshai knits his brows
Manohar Khyapa, will you ever be a Baul?
Threshing paddy yields the rice
What is threshing hay going to yield?
Love-water does not stay…

—Manohar Khyapa; Bengal

Practise It to Have It

Practise it to have it, seeker
Walk the talk
Till the practice intoxicates you
There is no real pleasure
Practise it to have it, seeker
Walk the talk

Blind men hold up torches
To point out the path
They lavish light on others
While plunged in the dark
Practise it…

A blind man doesn't look within
But gets called fine names
Puts on a show of generosity
Phony fulfilment and fame
Practise it…

Pundits and mullahs broke their heads
Tangled in the scripture
Who'll inform their eminences
Book-learning leaves you no wiser?
Practise it…

By guru's grace, in company of saints
Likhmo the gardener speaks
Does such a free-spirit exist
Who perfected his practice?
Practise it…

—Likhmo; Malwa

If You Want to Reach

O mad heart
If you want to reach
The land of Hari
Then lock up the room of attachments

Between still and moving
Flow upwards and be perfected
Embrace the feminine
Shed the curse of manhood
O mad heart…

Embody female energy
Rise to the higher self
O Shashanko, how many more days
Will you take
To become like a gopi?
O mad heart…

—Shashanko Goshai; Bengal

The Simple, Natural House

Do the simple, natural practice
In the simple, natural house
This practice can't be written down
It is beyond scriptures and ritual

If at the touch of fire
You can keep the butter from melting
Then form, union, joy flow upwards
Above the thirty-two chambers
Locked fast, requiring a key
The key is in the male and female
Form and taste
This main door opens on two sides
In the simple, natural house…

This main door which opens on two sides
Form, union and joy dwell there
One has to look quite carefully
To see the lord of joy seated there
He who is embodiment of that taste
Find the great feeling and become one form
Embodied drop and disembodied form
One who attains the groundless ground
In the simple, natural house…

The river of ardour, streaming towards Krishna
One drop of one wave of that river
Radha is the fully formed drop
The gopis are drops too
Who drip with the drops of devotion
While the world drains the drops of desire
In the simple, natural house…

Jaadu Bindu speak clearly
The inner feeling's the best path
Stay firm and certain
You'll see reality as it is
Countless ways, numberless books
That ocean will never dry
Though the tiny bird drinks endlessly
In the simple, natural house…

—Jaadu-Bindu; Bengal

Persuade Your Heart

Persuade your heart
Cajole your mind
To come to its senses
Sweet-talk it a bit!

Don't drink so much, brother
Don't smoke nor dope
These won't lead to absorption
You'll forget the drink of the Name
Brother, persuade your heart!

Don't make a bag of scriptures
Devotional songs, or mystic poetry
Don't pack a heavy suitcase
You'll miss the point
Brother, cajole your mind!

Such pure, clean eyes, brother
Don't deck them up with kohl
You'll distort their beauty
Brother, persuade your heart!

You carry a lamp, brother
If you forget it in the day
How will you pass the night?
Brother, cajole your mind!

Seated by her guru's feet
Roopabai says
I'm surrendered to Bhati, the master
Brother, persuade your heart!

—Roopabai; Malwa

No One Is Yours

No one is yours
Understand, O heart

Your wealth and gold
Your precious riches
A passing dream
Understand, O heart

We come naked
And leave naked
No covering remains
Understand, O heart

From between the brows
Life escapes
A shroud is put on the face
Understand, O heart

Four men act
As pall-bearers
They take you to the jungle
Understand, O heart

A fire is lit
On the bed of wood
You burn to dust
Understand, O heart

Kabir says
Listen seekers
That is our real home
Understand, O heart

—Kabir; Malwa

Why Wander Outside?

Your Raam is in your heart
Why wander outside?

Such rare gems hidden in the body
Who but a jeweller can know their worth?
Your Raam is in your heart
Why look outside?

Such pure ghee hidden in the milk
Will butter emerge without churning?
Your Raam is in your heart
Why wander outside?

Such bright flames hidden in the wood
Will fire ignite without friction?
Your Raam is in your heart
Why search outside?

Such big locks studded on the heart
Who but the guru can open these doors?
Your Raam is in your heart
Why wander outside?

Kabir says, listen seekers
Find Raam, then who can disturb you?
Your Raam is in your heart
Why look outside?

—Kabir; Rajasthan

Tear Out These Eyes

If with the first light of day
The beloved is not beheld
Tear out these eyes
Feed them to the crows

Keep your eyes exactly there
From where you can see your love
Don't look at anyone else
He gets easily upset, your love

Come and sit in my eyes
I'll shut the lids and hide you
The world will not see you
Nor I see anyone else

If you still see your self
There is no surrender
Lose the self
Then call out, Allah-u-Akbar!

—Shah Latif; Kutch (set of couplets)

The King's Head

Placing faith in Allah
The chaaran plucked his chang
Entranced jungle animals
Joined the gathering
May the lord not disappoint
Beejal in his quest

Placing faith in Allah
He came this way
He doesn't care for wealth
The beggar asks for my life!
Cut quickly now
I can't wait another second

Placing faith in Allah
He came this way
You soar higher than the sky
I crawl like a fool on earth
How can I woo you
Who delight only in heads?

The beggar entered the palace
Bearing his instrument
He struck up his melody
And fortresses fell

O Beejal, your music
Resounds everywhere
The cry has gone out in the city
You've asked for the king's head!

—Shah Latif; Kutch (set of couplets)

4. A SAVAGE MOCKERY

Human beings seem to have a persistent tendency to get caught up in outer ritual or form, and lose inner essence or meaning. Time and again, radical ideas and expressions of truth have arisen, but have been rapidly subverted or co-opted into orthodoxy. This is true not only of the history of religion, but also of more recent ideologies such as nationalism, liberalism or communism: the outer form persists but the essence gets corrupted, and begins ironically to mimic that which it set out to challenge.

Consider only this. Kabir, the great iconoclast, the incorrigible breaker of images, has himself been elevated to the status of god in several parts of north India, by people of a sect named after him—the Kabirpanthi group, which has many different, sometimes mutually warring, branches. These purported worshippers of Kabir have incorporated into their practices the very rituals and hierarchies that Kabir was mercilessly critical of, all without a hint of irony. Kabir is not the only one. Think of Jesus. Think of Marx.

Wherefrom comes this tendency? In a certain sense, it is easier to hold on to outer prescriptions than to the inner truth of a philosophy or practice. This is because while the inner truth is fluid and keeps shifting (because it is alive!), the outer form tends to remain stable and fixed (because it is dead). The mind finds it easier to grasp and cling to what seems unchanging and certain. The mind wants certainties. The mind deals in 'belief'. The mind worships dead things. In one song, Kabir describes the whole world as a 'village of the dead'.

In a very real sense, the place of truth can feel uncertain and insecure (from the perspective of the mind). It can be threatening. It forces you to not arrive at conclusions, to always stay alive to what is the truth of the moment. In the face of this, it is more comforting to hold fast to fixed forms and accepted beliefs. Hypocrisy has tended to be the favoured flavour of each age.

They bellow the azaan loudest
Whose hearts are the most corrupt
They make the journey for Haj
Whose crimes overflow at home
—Bulleshah

Accepted beliefs tend to accrue power to themselves. This is because the moment they take on an established tangible form, they become amenable to impulses of claiming, possessing, gate-keeping and legislating. Therefore there are vested interests behind setting up and maintaining orthodoxies. Over time, those who regulate and dispense these fixed beliefs become powerful authority figures. And they become extremely nervous and hostile to more dynamic and fluid voices.

This may be one reason why some Sufis (such as Issar Lal from Sindh) forbade their disciples from putting pen to their spoken verse and why Shah Latif is reputed to have thrown his poetry manuscripts into the river. Even a written poem may create an opportunity for orthodoxy.

The word orthodoxy comes from late Greek and means 'right opinion or belief'. The trouble begins when we begin to prescribe right opinions for everybody else. We also tend to ascribe orthodoxy only to others or to the past, because our own orthodoxies seem like natural truths to us. In the realms of religion, the 'orthodox' may be the clerics—the pundits, mullahs or gurus—but in other realms they could be politicians, academics, economists, doctors or...something closer home?

Kabir and other mystic poets bring an often-savage gaze to this human tendency, which can perhaps only be described as stupidity. Their poems bristle with ridicule, mockery and satire, hoping to jolt us out of our complacent ideas and our blindness to our own hypocrisies. Monks, ascetics, yogis, pundits, mullahs and even the Hindu gods are swept into the acerbic fold of their sarcasm.

Shiva, the trident-bearer, got looted!
Who will save his poor subjects?
—Kabir

Mystics are not against the use of startlingly blunt and confrontational language, in their desire to speak the truth. This is perhaps because they don't act out of fear.

Mullahs, shrine-keepers and pimps
They're all of the same ilk
They've sucked Allah dry
Like marrow from the bone
—Shah Latif

Such fiery critique of constructing orthodoxies around forms springs almost naturally from a thought-stream known as 'nirgun' (formlessness). The most favoured objects of attack are religion, ritual, caste and other hierarchical structures or mindless pursuits. But one must be careful. The mystics do not dismiss a higher power or greater truth altogether, as modern 'rationalists' or critics of old structures tend to do. They merely assert that it is somewhere else, to be reached or found in another way.

Divinity, or the truth, is repeatedly invoked as a phenomenon beyond name and form. It is called the Word, the Unseen, the Untraversed, the Unfragmented, the Unspeakable. Or, because it cannot be named, simply, the Name. But it is something very real. It is not a fancy. For the mystic, it is life, it is love itself.

There seems to be a real urgency behind the savageness of the attack and the uncompromising mockery. This urgency is a call to truth, a call to overcome all the pain, conflict, violence and suffering of the world, by finding a deeper place within oneself. The tone seems to be, 'Wake up! How can you be so stupid! The truth is staring you in the face!'

Hari isn't found by taking dips
It's easy to take baths!
Fish swim about in holy rivers
Do they make it to heaven?
—Bhavani Nath

We may chuckle and delight in these songs and poems, especially if the convictions they are mocking are not our own. But do we also get discomfited by them and begin to question, at least a little, some of our own conclusions?

The World Has Gone Mad

Seekers, look, the world has gone mad
If you speak the truth, they beat you up
If you speak falsehoods, they believe you

Hindus shout, Raam is ours!
Muslims shout, Rahman!
They die fighting each other
Neither understands the essence

I've met many a holy man
Who takes early morning baths
Meditates with pomp and show
His heart full of arrogance

Adorned with beads, caps, accessories
I've seen such gurus and holy men
They read the Qur'an and religious books
Take on disciples and show them graves
None of them come close to god

They mock me and laugh at me
And declare themselves wise and sane
Kabir says, listen seekers
Who among us is the mad one?

—Kabir; Urban

It's All Lies

What you say is all lies, dear preacher
What you speak is sheer deceit
If chanting 'Raam' brought salvation
Saying 'sugar' would have tasted sweet
It's all lies!

If limbs got burned by saying 'fire'
And crying 'water' appeased the thirsty
If shouting 'food' could take away hunger
The world would be saved already!
It's all lies!

Master and parrot both chant his name
With no real idea of Hari's glory
When the bird flies off to the forest
Hari no longer enters the story
It's all lies!

Without looking, without searching
What can be gained without the Name?
If saying 'money' made one millions
Which poor guy would stay the same?
It's all lies!

Your real love is your own desires
Hari-love falls to this fatal blow
Says Kabir, without meditation
Off in chains to death-city you go
It's all lies!

—Kabir; Malwa

Your Body's a City

Your body's a city, but who's the king?
Five robbers prowl on the highway
Five of them, twenty-five of them
Five bandits loot at will on the highway

Hope and desire, like a river in spate
Swept the greatest ascetics away
Those who swim upstream get saved
Signs are lit, pointing to the way
Your body's a city...

The naked forest hermit got fleeced
Craving stung him, hung him by his feet
He who didn't heed the guru
Troubles invaded that sage's retreat
Your body's a city...

Saints and devotees hijacked all paths
Reverend seekers on a twisted trip
Laying claims to the formless truth
Who can save them, O master of the ship!
Your body's a city…

When Indra seduced Gautama's wife*
Rama had to get her out of trouble
When Kubja** fell in love with Krishna
Radha and Rukmini were inconsolable
Your body's a city…

Shiva, the trident-bearer, got looted!
Who will save his poor subjects?
His troubled realm lost in forgetting
Even the gods get humbled in all ages
Your body's a city…

---

*Gautama Maharishi, one of the seven great Vedic sages, married Brahma's beautiful daughter, Ahilya. Indra, king of gods, taken by Ahilya's beauty, deceived Gautama into leaving the house for his morning prayers by making him think it was dawn when it was still night. He appeared to Ahilya in the form of Gautama and seduced her. Gautama discovered the deception upon his return and cursed both of them. Ahilya was turned into a rock. Later, the curse was revoked, and Ahilya was released when touched by Rama's feet on his way to Lanka.

**Kubja was a servant-girl who made perfumes in Kansa's palace in the *Bhagavata Purana*. She had a beautiful face but a hunched back. She gives Krishna an ointment meant for the king upon his asking, when they encounter each other on the streets of Mathura. Krishna relieves her of her deformities in return. She falls in love with Krishna and desires him. Later, Krishna visits her at her house and consummates her desire. Rukmini is Krishna's first wife, while Radha is his prime consort among the gopis. The song implies their jealousy, though it is not necessarily part of the legend.

Listen, Dharamdas, o true disciple
Kabir, the master, gives this call
The path is long, the way difficult
Remember the master creator of it all
Your body's a city…

—Dharamdas; Malwa

They've Sucked Allah Dry

Mullahs, shrine-keepers and pimps
They're all of the same ilk
They've sucked Allah dry
Like marrow from the bone

Don't call them 'mullahs'
They're hunters who sell
Sacred verses like pig's meat
They're a disgrace, says Latif

Don't call them 'mullahs'
God made them into donkeys
They beg and thieve to fill their bellies
Long after they're dead
God will still be angry

Don't call them 'mullahs'
They're blind as bats
Leave them to their debates
They read, but grasp nothing

—Shah Latif; Kutch (set of couplets)

You Lost Your Caste, They Shout

You lost your caste!
You've lost it, they shout
What a weird sweatshop this is!
No one's ready to do what's right
I've seen enough of this
Bogus business!

In the moment of coming
What caste were you?
Once here, which caste did you get?
What caste will you be
At the hour of death?
Did you figure out
This absurd plot yet?
You lost your caste, they shout!

Brahmin or gravedigger
Leather-worker or cobbler
The same water cleans them all
But no one's ready
To listen or see
Death spares no one, ah yes!
You lost your caste, they shout!

Secretly he visits a prostitute
But his piety suffers no blow
Lalon says, what the hell is 'caste'?
It's beyond my understanding, o yes
You lost your caste, they shout!

—Lalon Fakir; Bengal

Go Ask Your Guru

Go ask your guru
This voice speaking, whose is it?
Some say it's 'me'
Some say divinity
And if god lives within us
Then why do we get killed?

The spirit speaks in everything
Tree, water, forest, storm
Its play lies beyond the elements
It has neither colour nor form
Go ask…

Fort or hill provided the stone
You sculpted a beatific grin
But if the idol had any power
Wouldn't it rather feast on your skin?
Go ask…

Made-up gods speak through forms
The formless spreads everywhere
When the formless force awakens
These gods will bolt without a prayer
Go ask…

Kabir says, listen seekers
This path is without a map
One who searches out its ways
Slips out of duality's trap
Go ask…

—Kabir; Malwa

Where's Paradise, My Friend?

Where's paradise, my friend?
Where dwells the atom-sized truth
Where's that delight?

Snakes and asses laze around
None of them entered that mansion
How high is it, how big, how wide?
Can you tell how deep it runs?
Where's that paradise?

Never pricked your placid cow
Even took her to the Ganga for a dip
Wiped her tears with your own shirt
And forced more fodder down her lips!
Where's that paradise?

Almost halfway to heaven, swan
The temptress world pulled you back
The hag plunged you to the guts of hell
Re-hitched you to cycles of craving and lack
Where's that paradise?

What fine pots, what nice clothes
You've put on quite a show
But forgot the four fundamentals
Not a sliver of freedom you know
Where's that paradise?

This one's a Hindu, that one's a Muslim
Someone's a brahmin, another a trader
When the cage shatters, the parrot escapes
All difference fades into each other
Where's that paradise?

Facing-down you came, overturned you'll go
Flat on your belly on the pyre laid
Kabir says, birthed by reversal
What hope of being upright again
Where's that paradise?

—Kabir; Malwa

Leave Your Charades, O Yogi

You made a nice swing of banyan branches
O my precious yogi
But there's a fire under your butt!
Leave your charades and fake postures, O yogi
Be true in your practice
Be a real fakir

Hari isn't found by taking dips
It's easy to take baths!
Fish swim about in holy rivers
Do they make it to heaven?

Hari isn't found by shaving your head
Anyone can wield a razor!
Sheep get sheared every six months
Do they make it to heaven?

Hari isn't found by growing dreadlocks
It's easy to grow hair!
Bears in forests have thick hair
Do they make it to heaven?

I found my true guru, Gulabi Nath
And now my heart feels whole
Take me across with your call
Bhavani Nath sings your glory

—Bhavani Nath; Rajasthan

O Mullah, What Would You Know?

O mullah, what would you know
Of Muhammad's glory?
If you want to know
Go ask Hussain or Uwais
Or Bilal or Ali of Karbala
Enough of your cheap tricks
Your wanton ways
What use are your endless prayers
If your heart doesn't bow
In reverence?

*

They do the namaaz
Who are weak of heart
They keep the ritual fast
Who are stingy with bread
They bellow the azaan loudest
Whose hearts are the most corrupt
They make the journey for Haj
Whose crimes overflow at home
Says Bulleshah, do you want to meet god?
Then simply unlock
The chamber of your heart!

*

Reading book after book
You've become a great scholar
But you never learnt to read yourself
You go rushing
Into temples and mosques
But never enter your own heart
Every day you fight the devil
But never wrestle
With your own ego
You chase after those in the sky
But never look for
The one sitting at home

—Bulleshah; Rajasthan (set of couplets)

You Didn't Sing Govind's Name

You didn't sing Govind's name
What did you earn, O foolish one?
What did you really gain?

You steal a slab of iron
And give a needle in charity
Then you climb the roof to see
Why isn't applause coming to me?
You didn't sing Govind's name…

A 'Hindu', yet you cut the peepal tree
Live on your daughter's pay
A 'Muslim', yet you demand interest
Your capital is frittered away
You didn't sing Govind's name…

You take dips in Ganga and Gomti
And climb the holy Girnar
Like the weary bullock of a gypsy
Waste your life wandering around
You didn't sing Govind's name...

Sitting in a boat made of stone
You set sail on the river
Says Kabir, listen friends
You're sure to drown midway
You didn't sing Govind's name...

—Kabir; Rajasthan

These Guys Know Nothing

These guys know nothing
They know nothing at all
They don't value this rosary
They wear it for a while
Turn it for a while
Then throw it in the ditch!

Once a dog was shown a mirror
He stopped dead in his tracks
Tried to peer inside and outside
Turning tail, he barked and fled!
These guys know nothing...

Once a monkey discovered a pearl
He had no idea what it was!
Is it sweet or salty, he wondered
And rubbed his mouth in the mud!
These guys know nothing...

A necklace was put on a buffalo's neck
Does she understand its worth?
Swaying her hips, she waddles off
To roll about in the slush!
These guys know nothing…

An ass was taken to the Ganga
Will the holy dip purify him?
Says Kabir, listen seekers
He'd rather be in a garbage dump!
These guys know nothing…

—Kabir; Malwa

Who Cares for You, Formless God?

Who cares for you, formless god?
No one serves you, unfabricated deity
No one prays to you

They flock at the banks of form
Perform all kinds of ritual
The master is whole and unfragmented
They can't solve this riddle
Who cares for you…?

The heads of Brahma, Vishnu, Shiva
Are thickly blighted over with moss
Don't rely on such fellows who
Themselves didn't make it across!
Who cares for you…?

The ten avatars are transient gods
Hardly equipped to save us
They're stuck in cycles of karma
The real doer is nameless
Who cares for you…?

Yogis, sadhus, ascetics, monks
Bicker idly among themselves
Kabir says, listen seekers
Glimpse the Word, get out of this mess
Who cares for you…?

—Kabir; Malwa

The Fish Is Thirsty in Water

O seeker
The fish is thirsty in water!
I laugh when I hear
The fish is thirsty in water

Without self-knowledge, you wander
What use Mathura or Kashi?
The deer has musk in its belly
But roams the forest desperately

He whom even Hari contemplates
And countless other yogis
That one sits in your very body
Supreme undying being

Lotus in water, buds in the lotus
When the bee dwells on this flower
Mind, mastered, embraces all worlds
And becomes a true renunciant

What's right here, you call far away
All talk of 'far away' is fruitless
Kabir says, listen seeker
Only the guru can shatter illusion

—Kabir; Malwa

5. THE WORLD AS MARKETPLACE

Even though we live in quite soulless 'market economy' times, where even emotions form part of commercial trade (think social media or advertising), in our hearts perhaps we still cling to a somewhat more poetic description of life and the world. Surely, it is all about love and beauty and spirit and whatnot.

These poets, contrary to what we might expect, take a starkly differing point of view. To be in this world is to be in a state of transaction. Everything is trade or exchange. In-breath and out-breath. Consumption and excretion. Acquisition and expenditure. Even physical intimacy.

To give and to take: this is emphasized as a basic fact of life. And yet, the inevitability of transacting is not understood in purely commercial terms, as we tend to do these days. The entire universe is based on exchange! Mass and energy. Push and pull. Earth and sun. The moon and the tides.

Everything responds to everything else—this is a different way of understanding transaction, or exchange. We are constantly taking in and giving out. It is the very fabric of life.

And so the poetry describes the seeker as a saudaagir, a merchant or trader. We're all traders here. The world is a marketplace. Life is transaction.

But what kind of transaction? What is the quality of our trade? And are there different possibilities? In one of his iconic sonnets, Wordsworth famously says:

The world is too much with us; late and soon,
Getting and spending, we lay waste our powers;
Little we see in Nature that is ours;
We have given our hearts away, a sordid boon!

Kabir says we must choose the kind of shop we will set up, decide on the kind of trade we will engage in. At the end of the day, we will have to reckon our profits and our losses.

Kabir, the shop is shut
All transactions done
You filled your bag with counterfeits
And can't touch the real anymore

Many songs speak of the 'deal'. It's important to get a good deal, strike the right bargain. To be acutely aware of one's jewels (of each breath), to make the most of each possibility (each moment of consciousness), to not fritter one's capital (energy, attention) away—this is the essence of good business sense.

O swan
In the city of the body-self
You'll find an upside-down market!
Become a jewel-trader, swan
And strike a priceless bargain

We are in this world. We are here to transact, exchange, participate. And yet, how to be in the world and not of it? Shah Latif puts this wonderfully well in one particular couplet:

The beloved tied me up
And flung me into the sea
Standing on the shore, he said
Watch out, don't get your clothes wet!

The 'world' is often described in this poetry as bhavsaagar or an ocean of becoming. Everything is in a state of transience, of becoming something else, in a mode of transition from its current state to some other state. Nothing is fixed. Nothing is still. Everything is ever-changing, like the surface of the ocean.

And so the advice is—on the one hand, to touch the stillness of the depths, where the pearl is formed; and on the other, to ride these waves, instead of getting smashed against the rocks by them. The journey of being in the world is one of going through all the cycles of human experience—craving, aversion, gain, loss, worry, fear, satisfaction, desire, regret, despair, weariness. And is there another kind of experience beyond this?

What kind of trader are we, dealing in what goods, having set up what kind of shop? To what do we give our attention away? And what do we harvest in return?

Row Along the Banks of This River

Row along the banks of this river
O merchant-mind
I'll reveal the secrets of your heart
O merchant-heart

Born into this world
I carry no desires with me
At both dawn and dusk I light
A lamp filled with the oil of desires
O merchant-mind

Like a flame leaps towards the sky
I made a wick of my ego
And lit just one, a single lamp
That lights up the whole world
O merchant-heart

Hamsa* flows down the river
Over which you too have passed
She drinks its milk but not its water
For she has known the supreme
O merchant-mind

—'Hamsa' (Parvathy Baul); Bengal

The Cup Is Full

Your cup is full with Raam-nectar, O bee
Don't go thirsty!

This nectar can't be priced or sold
It flows freely through the year
One on the path drinks her fill
The aimless one goes thirsty
O bee, don't go thirsty!

The market is set up to trade
Transact any amount you like
The trader struck a good bargain
The fool wears a long face
O bee, don't go thirsty!

---

*'Hamsa' is the poetic pen name adopted by the contemporary Baul singer and practitioner, Parvathy Baul. The 'hamsa' or 'hans' is the swan or the goose, who is mythologically reputed to drink only milk and eat only pearls.

Each balance is the same
Be a saint and see it
Weigh on the scale of the self
Nobody lacks anything
O bee, don't go thirsty!

The riches of Raam brim over
Be smart and taste them
Kabir says, listen secret-knower
The fool goes thirsty
O bee, don't go thirsty!

—Kabir; Malwa

Drink the Wine of Hari's Name

O swan
Let's go to the guru's country
Where the crow turns into a swan
Where lightning flashes
And rain falls unceasingly

O swan
Drink the wine of Hari's name
Cycles of becoming will end
Drink from the cup of fearlessness

O swan
A sandalwood plough tills the field
Sow the seeds of jewels in it
Harvest the pearls of Hari's name
Watered by true seekers and saints
Drink the wine of Hari's name

O swan
A crop of pearls lies in the field
But the world steps over it
When the knower of its worth arrives
It sells for a handsome price
Drink the wine of Hari's name

O swan
In the city of the body-self
You'll find an upside-down market!
Become a jewel-trader, swan
And strike a priceless bargain
Drink the wine of Hari's name

O swan
Know Hari in every breath
No delay in it, no searching
Dev Dungarpuri says
This is a moment of true fortune
Drink the wine of Hari's name

—Dev Dungarpuri; Kutch

If You Wish to Receive

If you wish to receive, do so now
Now is the hour for receiving, O seeker!
This human birth is hard to attain
Stumbling through endless cycles of being
This priceless gem may not come around again

The dark hair of your youth has turned grey
But has that made you mend your ways?
Good actions, not good words, bring grace
One who transforms does not go astray
This human birth…

You blabber fine words—do you live them?
What good is such wisdom, unlived?
Will it quench a thirsty heart's seeking?
Won't you wander again, lost, unhinged?
This human birth...

Swan, walk with the gait of a swan
No stepping in shallow puddles anymore!
Light pervades the seeker's whole body
Alone, with art, she plays, she sports
This human birth...

Head taken off and placed before the guru
No room for doubt anymore, O seeker
Collecting the five, I made them one
Experience lies within the self, O seeker
This human birth...

When grace appeared, the bargain was struck
And Rohal made off with the priceless jewel
Now what need of adulation or fame?
He cut off his head, and became immortal
This human birth...

—Rohal Fakir; Rajasthan

My Darling Awareness

O my artful awareness
O my darling awareness
Fill your cup with the wine of Raam
Have Raam's name on your lips
Rend the inner veil
O my darling awareness

Fall in love with the navel-lotus
My true guru's set up a shop
Trade there in the feeling of devotion
You'll get dyed in all colours
O my artful awareness

Take a walk in the vast sky-dome
Enter the master's palace
Jewels grow in the jewel-city
You'll find a diamond
O my artful awareness

Climb the vast sky-circle
Riding on the master's strength
Light shimmers, comes pouring down
You'll scale the impassable pass
O my artful awareness

Fall in love with the name of Raam
Such is Bhakturam's request
Beyond seventeen lands a land*
There the yogi rests
O my artful awareness

—Bhakturam; Malwa

Why?

Why?
Trapped in craving and fear,
Desire and aversion?
Why?

*Prahlad Tipanya, a well-known Malwi folk singer, says that this may refer to the seventeen vertebrae between the navel and nostrils where the breath normally travels up and down.

His own meat
Is the deer's worst enemy
Not a moment's peace
From Bhusuku the hunter
Why?

He eats no grass
Drinks no water
The deer who's lost the way
To the doe's house
Why?

The doe says, listen deer
Quit this forest, run like mad
So fast that your feet
Can't be seen
Says Bhusuku,
Fools don't get this truth
Why?

—Bhusuku; Bengal

My Business Is with God

From clan, family, children
Hope of worldly gain and wealth
If by meditating on Hari
All this breaks, let it break

My business is with god
If the world gets upset
Let it agitate

Mingling with true seekers
Let me earn well-being
If the world is engrossed
In pleasure, let it luxuriate
My business is with god

Focusing attention on god
My heart became absorbed
If love for worldly objects
Comes to an end, let it fade
My business is with god

A pot of sins held over my head
My great guru brought it down
Brahmanand flung it to the ground
If it breaks, let it break
My business is with god

—Brahmanand; Rajasthan

6. THE TRUTH OF SUFFERING

There is sorrow. There is a cause for sorrow. There is a way to relieve the cause for sorrow. This way is the eightfold path.

This is how the Buddha formulated the four noble truths upon his enlightenment. The first noble truth seems harsh, yet inescapable. There is sorrow.

Who can deny it? In moments of despair, we might find that the whole world is afflicted by sorrow—some overt, some hidden away carefully. Often, we seem to seek pleasure only to forget pain.

The day spent in eating
The night in sleep
Human birth is so precious
You traded it for nothing
—Kabir

In this tradition, the greatest (and most useful) form of suffering is self-recognition. To finally, clearly, see oneself in the mirror. This is not at all a pleasant encounter. What we behold is not a pretty sight. Habituated as we are to finding faults outside, turning the gaze upon oneself can be painful. All our lives, the truths about our personalities that we seek to escape from keep coming back to haunt us. Our partners or children or associates keep pointing them out to us. Or life brings us situations where our own role in our own and others' misery becomes undeniable. Even Kabir is forced to acknowledge his shortcomings to his guru, Ramanand.

I can't hide from my follies
I recognize my own failings
Ramanand, I messed up

There is also the larger, undeniable reality of suffering. Of course, life affords a lot of pleasures and joys to each person on their own unique path. But it is futile to try to deny the truth of suffering. Often we are left bewildered by death, disease, loss, old age, or sudden misfortune. Suffering then has the potential to become the first doorway into something more than oneself—it carries the possibility of opening us up to something larger than the pursuit of one's own gratifications.

Rabindranath Tagore says in *Gitanjali*:

> My desires are many and my cry is pitiful, but ever didst thou save me by hard refusals; and this strong mercy has been wrought into my life through and through.[12]

The pain of passing, of ephemerality, of impermanence, of death, dogs us. And yet we cling, desperately, to our attachments. Non-fulfilment of desire is experienced as sorrow. The wish to hang on to something or someone that wants or has to leave is experienced as pain. There is the agony of loss. Each loss brings its own unique grief. Slowly, through painful learning, perhaps we learn to unclench, at least a little.

There's a bankruptcy that's pure gain.
The moon stays bright when it
doesn't avoid the night.

A rose's rarest essence
lives in the thorn.
—Rumi[13]

In a way, sorrow can be the path. It makes us wake up to ourselves. As Kabir says in one song, wealth and family bring pleasure, but also forgetfulness. Sorrow brings us back to awareness. Perhaps it doesn't need to be like this, yet this is how it is. In a curious formulation expressing this truth, Eckhart Tolle says that suffering is necessary until it is no longer necessary. In other words, suffering becomes unnecessary once we consent to staying awake without the needle of suffering.

Using a famous love-legend from Sindh and Punjab, Shah Latif speaks of the grief of Sasui, who loses her husband on her wedding night.

Sasui is a brahmin girl abandoned at birth by her parents and raised in a town called Bhambhor by a childless Muslim washerman and washerwoman. Her crime is to fall in love with a stranger called Punhu, who is a prince, son of King Aari Jaam of Ketch, from across the desert. For this crime, her punishment is to have her husband abducted on the night of her wedding, right after the nuptials! Before Punhu can reach Sasui awaiting him in the bridal chamber, he is plied with alcohol by his brothers in the name of festivity. In the dead of the night, Punhu is put on to their camels and taken across the desert, back to where he came from. Sasui, when she awakes, sets off alone across the hot desert, without any supplies, in the pursuit of her retreating beloved.

Her family and friends try to stop her from embarking on this impossible journey. She brushes them off with the conviction that the beloved is not found without striving and suffering. This might sound like a strange thing to say—the beloved is found in grief. But pride needs shattering. Attachments need rupturing. Forgetfulness needs rude awakening. Suffering, if we let it, is what may lead us out of suffering.

The destination is not clear
And I haven't carried any water
The mountain path is cruel
The desert sun is harsh
Beloved, come to me there
Where I'm most alone with my grief
—Shah Latif

Look What I've Done

A spotless pot with pure, cool water
I threw away all that water
Ramanand, look what I've done

I can't hide from my follies
I recognize my own failings
Ramanand, I messed up

I kept the cow from drinking water
Separated her from her calf
Ramanand, look what I've done

I've seen endless ages pass
At each step, a mistake
Ramanand, I messed up

I snatched the brahmin's bowl
I tore apart his books
Ramanand, look what I've done

Kabir says, listen seekers
I surrender my head at your feet
Ramanand, I messed up

—Kabir; Rajasthan

Youth and Wealth

Youth and wealth are passing guests
To be vain is foolishness

A frame made of bones and flesh
With a deep pool of water
Bewitching colours on the surface
God, the fabricator
To be vain is foolishness

Animal skin gets used in shoes
In drums and tambourines
But your skin is useless, Man
Your pride burnt to ashes
To be vain is foolishness

Ten heads and twenty arms
Wealth, powers, a big clan
Conceit wrecked even such a man
The king and chief of Lanka
To be vain is foolishness

The world is a dream fabric
Act with virtue and wisdom
Says Kabir, listen seekers
Cross the ocean of becoming
To be vain is foolishness

—Kabir; Rajasthan

The Disease Called Worry

Is there a cure in this world
For the disease called worry?
Tell me, friends

Worry in the day, worry at night
In the afternoon, worry
Even if I leave worries
Worry never leaves me
Tell me, friends...

Even fire is better than worry
It burns only the dead
But worry burns you alive
When you're in the grip of it
Tell me, friends...

Shorot says, worry spared
No one in this world
So worry over with that which
Will free you of worldly worries
Tell me, friends...

—Shorot; Bengal

How Frail Your Body

How frail your body, how false your world
How untrue the account you give of it
O Raam, dear Raam
Pray tell, do tell
Who fabricated your frail body?

In the body, Ganga flows
In the body, Yamuna flows
In the body, the pilgrim who takes the dip
O Raam, dear Raam
Pray tell…

In the body, the lock
In the body, the key
In the body, the one who opens the door
O Raam, dear Raam
Pray tell…

In the body, the ripe mango
In the body, the raw mango
In the body, the one who tastes and knows
O Raam, dear Raam
Pray tell…

With Machhinder's grace
Gorakh says
One who got this, got everything
O Raam, dear Raam
Pray tell…

—Gorakhnath; Malwa

Friends, Be on Your Way

Friends, be on your way
My destiny is written
I'm bound to Punhu

Allah Miyan
Put shackles on the feet
Of the camels of Aari Jaam
My fate is sealed

Allah Miyan
In the city of Bhambhor
Hear the plea of this poor wretch
My destiny is written

Allah Miyan
Shah Latif says, listen friends
The thirst within me is intense
My fate is sealed

—Shah Latif; Kutch

The Mountain Burst into Flames

Sasui's grief is immense
She weeps at every step
She's crossed mountains
No trace of Punhu's footsteps

The mountain burst into flames
When it brushed against my pain
O friend, the earth was scorched
There is no more hope
Of life in my mind

Friends, a barren desert lies ahead
Don't think of coming with me
For one, there is no water
Second, the path is long and desolate
You'll curse my Punhu
When you perish on the way

—Shah Latif; Kutch (set of couplets)

7. LONGING

Wanting.
Having.
Wanting.

We are all too familiar with the experience of 'wanting'. To want is to be in a place of lack. To miss or need something or someone, to feel incomplete. In an age when we are mostly defined by what we have—money, possessions, knowledge, opinions, awards, achievements, relationships—the condition of wanting is almost like an epidemic. If we have this, we lack that. If we get that, we want something else. And so on.

Then there is the so-called 'having'—mostly a momentary and fleeting sense of satisfaction at getting what we want, before we fall into wanting again. Owning, possessing, deriving one's identity out of something, one tries to become 'more' by adding more things or experiences or accreditations to one's personality. The more one 'has', the more one imagines one will feel secure.

Actually, the reverse may be true. Having itself gives rise to all kinds of insecurity: fear of loss, of competition, of usurpation, of future irrelevance…

Away from this mundane cycle of wanting-having-wanting, the mystic cries out for another state of being.

Travelling under the hot desert sun of Balochistan on the way to Mecca on a pilgrimage, the Sufi poet Shah Latif and his friend came upon the sight of thirsty buffaloes rushing to slake their thirst in a lake. On drinking their fill, they relieved themselves in the same lake. Then they turned their backs on it and walked away. Shah Latif was deeply struck by this incident and abandoned his pilgrimage. It made him reflect on viraha, the state of separation and longing. He composed the following poem in that moment, resolving to cultivate the restless fire of longing, not the cool complacency and negligence that might follow satisfaction.

I long and long for you
But may you never be mine
I yearn and cry for you
Beloved, always stay apart from me

This longing is not about desire and its gratification. This longing is to be in the throes of an intensity which is its own painful reward, its own sweet punishment. It has a special edge. It is not for particular things; indeed, it is not for any 'thing'. It is a state to be cultivated for its own sake. Again, Latif says:

As long as you give me life
Keep me thirsting for you
Free of all created things
Hankering for nothing but you

The impulse here is to give oneself up, to go beyond the wants of the hungry personality. There is perhaps a small self in all of us, which is like the shell of an egg. Inside, there is another being longing to break out, to transcend its limitations. This is a very different taste from trying to expand oneself by adding to the personality through accruing things, achievements or 'followers'.

This longing may be expressed in many ways. It is the yearning for Krishna, the 'Dark One'. It is the desperate call for the 'Beloved'. It is the endless waiting for the 'friend'. It is the utter surrender to the 'guru'.

'Viraha is a way of detaching yourself from the world,' says Parvathy Baul. 'Being dispassionate is being very passionate. When one is one-pointed in one's love for the Beloved, it's a very passionate state of being, and one becomes dispassionate about the world.'

It is strange to think that longing and detachment are the very same thing. Or, indeed, that passion and dispassion may be the same thing. A man of the world, rich, successful, admired, respected, liked, begins to long for something else. He cannot explain it. Everything that people desire, hanker for, he has. And yet he is not happy. There is an ache in his heart. He gets restless. He cannot go on anymore. He yearns for something else. He knows not what it is, or even if his longing is for something real. And yet, he cannot help himself. He flings off all his expensive robes and steps into the field of a bewildering search, a fiery thirst. This is the beginning of viraha.

It is a kind of fire, which burns away everything apart from itself. No one imagines that this kind of thing will bring them happiness. Instead, this longing brings restlessness, thirst, and the pain of separation. It makes you confront yourself. It is real suffering, a fire which cleanses and refines, a kind of fever. You lose your appetite and your sleep. You experience helplessness, powerlessness, and an irrepressible urge to plead, demand, petition and beseech. It transforms you without your being able to help yourself—which is, perhaps, the only way that our personalities will agree to transform.

Everyone says they're moved, they're struck
But 'being struck' is a terrible thing
Say you're struck only when
The sword has cut you through and through
—Kabir

I Haven't Met My Love

I haven't met my love
This day too has passed
Love took me
This maddened, blind creature
Death came on the road
With the beloved's name on my lips

I haven't met my love
A thousand suns have set
Let me see him once
Then give up my breath

I haven't met my love
And you are setting, sun
Take this message to my love
Go tell them in Ketch
Wretched thing
She died on the path

I haven't met my love
The sun is dangling upside down
The fault is mine
I let him slip through my fingers
He didn't take me with him
To his country

I haven't met my love
The sun has reached its setting
I will light on this dark mountain
A lamp for my Baroch
I want no life
Without him, my friends!

—Shah Latif; Kutch (set of couplets)

To Attain Your Holy Feet

Just to attain your holy feet
This wretch calls out your name
From the depths of time

From my own past created
For what fault was I plunged
Into the cycle of becoming?
Brought, with what thought,
To this abject state where I forget
Your compassionate name?

You bear the name of wish-fulfilling tree
So the clan of ascetics told me
Why be renowned as compassionate
If you can't help me be free?

I fail to remember Heeruchand's feet
Heedless Panjushah says
Is this your famed compassion
That you don't let me near your feet?

—Panjushah; Bengal

O Dark One, Come Quickly

Come quickly, O Raam
Come soon, O Hari
Beads of my rosary
Crafter of my body
Come as soon as you can!

Why this delay, O dark one?
Come quickly, O Raam!
Beads of my rosary
Come soon, O dark one

For you, for you
The tank has been filled
Come and bathe, lord
Come swiftly
I stand here waiting
O master, come quickly

For you, for you
I've cooked all this food
Come and feast, lord
Come swiftly
I've been waiting a long time
Take note of my presence
O dark one, come quickly

For you, for you
The pitcher has been filled
Come and drink, lord
Come swiftly
Beads of my rosary
I've been waiting for ages
Register my attendance
O master, come quickly

With humility, Gorakh says
Keep my honour, don't let me down
O master, come swiftly
I'm waiting for you
O dark one, come quickly

—Gorakhnath; Malwa

The Yogis Cast a Spell on Me

The yogis cast a spell on me
My body and heart are theirs

Restless days and sleepless nights
Like a wounded deer I whimper
The Word-arrow has pierced my flesh
My frame lies shattered
The yogis cast a spell…

I think of neither food nor drink
In the grief of constant yearning
The world's lost its sweetness for me
I've found the drink of love
The yogis cast a spell…

Longing-fire burns my flesh
It melts the mirage of differences
Love-elation is taking over
My heart is drenched with love
The yogis cast a spell…

Peacock-feather crown and garland
I got a glimpse of my Krishna
He's taken Suabai across
Wasn't this the purpose of living?
The yogis cast a spell…

—Suabai; Rajasthan

My Heart Aches

My heart aches
Without my beloved

Fretful days, sleepless nights
Tossing and turning the dawn arrives
My heart aches
Bereft of my beloved

Mind and body in a whirl
A wasted life on a vacant bed
My heart's in torment
Without my beloved

Kabir says, listen seekers
Hari rid me of these sorrows
My heart aches
Bereft of my beloved

—Kabir; Sindh

Krishna, Do You Ever Think of Me?

O Krishna, do you think of me at all?
Tell me, Krishna
Do you ever remember me?
Alas, I adore even your forgetfulness

Tell me, O Krishna
O my dear Krishna
I remember every little trifle
Whether you remember or not!
Do you ever think of me?

I pestered the priest with entreaties
For each moment's news of you
I fell at the feet of Shiva
Even magic charms have failed!
Do you ever think of me?

To hell with this dratted marriage
I was better off being single!
I lived in peace in my parents' home
Why did I run about after you?
Do you ever think of me?

Why did I go all crazy for you, O Krishna?
Do you ever think of me?

—Nawab Sadiq Jung Bahadur 'Hilm'; Sindh

Can't Be Alone at Home Anymore

Monsoon rains are here, my friend
Pouring down
I can't be alone at home anymore
I long to meet my beloved
Tell me, how will I survive this?

Pitter-patter, water falls, dear friend
It won't listen to me
Separated from Shyam
Water pours from my eyes
How will I survive this?

Peacocks and peahens dance, dear friend
They dance in bliss
Salavat says, once gone
These days won't return again
How will I survive this?

—Salavat Mahato; Bengal

I'm Not at Peace for a Moment

I'm not at peace for a moment
Without you, my love
Alone, my heart is restless
Without you, my love

May no one's lover
Leave for distant lands
May no one face the sorrow of parting
I'm not at peace for a moment

Your absence is agony
Sorrows are a thousand!
Every day is apocalypse
For the separated ones
I'm not at peace for a moment

O crow, I'll give you a sugar treat
Come sit on my window ledge
Bring me news from my beloved
I'll shower you with blessings
I'm not at peace for a moment

My nights are lit
With a lamp of my tears
O god, unite me now
With my beloved!
I'm not at peace for a moment

—Unknown; Rajasthan, Punjab, Sindh

Because of You

I gave up my home and hearth
Because of you
I plunged into the ocean
With the hope
Of finding a pearl

O friend!
I am crazy about you
The whole world knows
You've struck a dagger
In this wretch's heart
O cold-hearted one
Because of you…

O friend!
Sorrows are my path
I can't hope for joy
I roam from here to there
The dream of union slips away
Like water from my eyes
Because of you…

O friend!
I went to the river
And told it of my sorrows
The water evaporated!
I went to the tree
And told it of my suffering
It shed all its leaves!
Because of you…

—Unknown; Bengal

8. THE COMPANY WE KEEP

Are we wholly individual beings, encased in our sovereign bodies and minds, impervious to the influence of others and of our surroundings? Are our thoughts and emotions exclusively *our* thoughts and emotions, properly belonging to us, manufactured by our own exclusive heart and mind?

In other words: are we solid, substantial selves, separate from our environment? Or are we somewhat porous entities, not so well-encased as we think, not as autonomous and independent as we imagine?

Do we somehow think and feel through osmosis, by absorbing subtle or gross influences from the atmosphere, and from each other?

The 20th century can perhaps be described as a century of mass mania, given the number of genocides, holocausts, large-scale wars and nuclear and chemical warfare that occurred. But instances of mass madness and irrationality have been common throughout history. How do we explain this phenomenon except as an infection of thought—a reflection of how the current of the particular age or time proves to be stronger than the individual?

These are perhaps two distinct models of conceptualizing the human being. The unique 'modern individual' imagines herself to be the progenitor and possessor, the owner and creator, of her thoughts, emotions and actions. She is a world unto herself.

A more ancient kind of tradition insists that we are very much impacted by our aahaar, that is, by all the inputs we consciously or unconsciously take in. A Hindi saying goes: *Jaisa anna, vaisa mann* (as the food is, so is the mind).

The idea of food is not limited only to what we consume through our mouths. Food is also the company we keep, the places we visit, the media we consume, the thoughts and feelings we dwell on, our sights, our smells, our sounds. In this way of understanding the human being, how we think and feel is deeply linked with the environment we are in. Be with a clever person and your cleverness increases. Spend time with a kind person, and perhaps you will become more kind.

Is it any wonder then that this tradition places so much emphasis on satsang? Satsang literally means the company of truth. Practically, it translates to the ideas and people we hang out with. To listen to words of truth is already a kind of food. It is a food we direly need. To keep company of the baser emotions—greed, fear, jealousy, anger—is another kind of food.

Satsang is not only the kind of people we mingle with, but also hanging out with elevating ideas, inspiring words, uplifting music. The German writer Goethe expresses this as the statement of a very modest ambition: 'One ought, every day at least, to hear a little song, read a good poem, see a fine picture, and, if it were possible, to speak a few reasonable words.'

The contemporary Hind-Urdu poet Nida Fazli expresses this in a verse:

In good company,
a person is transformed
Like the kiss of a mango
makes the sunlight sweeter

In a song with a haunting refrain—Whom should I love, o friend?—an iconic story of love is narrated in a matter of a few verses. A bird is in love with the tree on which it lives. When a fire breaks out in the dry season and engulfs the whole forest, all the birds and animals begin to flee. But this little bird goes to a nearby pond, dips herself, comes back over the tree, and flaps her wings. A few drops of water fall… And so she continues. The fire rages over the whole forest. The bird pursues her unrelenting effort.

The power of her love stuns the entire universe. So much so that the gods are moved, and begin to weep. And in this song, the weeping gods bring about a rain of milk. The song shows emphatically that satsang is also love. We grow into the image of what we stay with. What we stay with is what we love.

A culture where we are encouraged to consume indiscriminately is perhaps based on the belief that there is not much intercourse between our outer and inner worlds, that our minds and hearts can stay more or less untouched by their interactions with the outside. No matter what we eat or watch or hear or think, we will not be impacted. These songs suggest the very opposite; that we are deeply vulnerable—both to the power of love and truth, as well as to the influences of hate, indifference and untruth.

Just as we are learning these days to choose our food with care, in that there are choices ranging from junk food to artisanal, homegrown produce, so we might also choose the food of our mind. Whom do we listen to? What do we let our senses consume? To what do we expose our consciousness?

We are given the discretion to choose.

Not for Half-baked Ones

Friend, let's welcome the saints who are here
The heart's secret is not for half-baked ones
Lift the veil if a wholehearted one appears
Girl, let's cherish the seekers gathered here

Friend, don't hang out in bad company
Where your dignity is diminished
Girl, keep the company of truth
Where your worth is embellished
Friend, let's welcome...

Friend, how different one man from another
One, a conch, the other, a hollow shell
Girl, how different one well from another
One is brackish, the other sweetness itself
Friend, let's welcome...

Friend, your ocean has tiny wellsprings
Whose water is sweet and clear
Says Kabir to Dharamdas
Hold the guru close, keep him near
Friend, let's welcome...

—Dharamdas; Kutch

Whom Should I Love?

Whom should I love, my friend?
True seekers make for good company
Seek the kinship of the pure in heart

A bamboo plant grew in this forest
The whole forest trembled
It burns itself and everything around it
So much fire in its belly!

A sandalwood tree grew in this forest
The whole forest rejoiced
I go near the sandalwood tree
I become fragrant too!

Fire engulfs the whole forest
A bird comes and sits on the tree
I have no wings, I must burn
But you save yourself and fly away!

I ate your fruit, I soiled your leaves
I played from branch to branch
You burn, and I fly away?
You live and love but once!

The fire was extinguished
The clouds rained milk
Says Kabir to Dharamdas,
Each moment my love is new

—Dharamdas; Rajasthan

Keep Swan-Company

Keep swan-company to be a swan
If all you do is mingle with herons
Who will recognize you, swan?
Keep swan-company to be a swan

The swan lives in the lake of milk
No lakes of water there
Those lakes are attachment-water
Give this up to be a swan
Keep swan-company…

Ten divinities, six philosophies
Reading all these reams of text
Caste, categories, and holy scripture
Give this up to be a swan
Keep swan-company…

The five mantra-names are unreliable
They won't get you freedom
Quit this crowd, meet the true guru
Liberation will be simple
Keep swan-company...

Yogis enter their temples drunk
Clueless about the path
Holy men only in appearance
With no idea of the One
Keep swan-company...

Death-king rules over all worlds
He loves fitting out his arrows
Walk with care on your path, O swan
And death will admit defeat
Keep swan-company...

The deathless city's the swan's abode
Not this endless cycle of becoming
Kabir says, listen seekers
My true guru showed me the sign
Keep swan-company...

—Kabir; Malwa

9. KEEP IT TO YOURSELF!

How thrilling it can be to know a secret, have a secret, keep a secret! But there are some secrets we don't want to keep. There are areas in which we want publicity rather than privacy. In many places, we want to broadcast ourselves, we do not want to stay hidden. In contemporary India, for example, loudspeakers noisily announce the (decibel) levels of our piety. It seems our devotion is not true devotion until we can batter the other person into acknowledging it! In new-age circles there are careless-seeming but carefully-framed comments about the richness of our yoga practice, our meditational excitements or spiritual pursuits. It seems like even our religiosity or spiritual practice or inner work has to be certified by others.

There is one kind of impulse in us—to communicate, to share an insight or inspiration, to get something across. When it is to a worthy recipient, it could lead to an experience of communion. Something grows richer through exchange. Sometimes the teacher learns more while teaching.

But there is also another kind of impulse in us which is to seek validation for our experiences, or our very existence, from others. We express not so much in order to communicate our truth, but in order to be assured that we are right, and good, and worthy. We do it for show, to proclaim ourselves, to assert our authority over something. Outwardly, the two impulses may look alike. Only the seeker knows the true inner state, the real motivation.

When we express in order to prove ourselves or to seek

validation, we give our power away. How does this happen (if it does)? We become dependent on the response. We don't trust our own experience unless it is validated. And even if validation comes once, we need it over and over again, because now our strength lies in the validation, not in the experience itself.

In effect, perhaps we have lost the experience. This can be a difficult idea, especially in a culture so given over to show and tell. When everyone endorses the pursuit of securing an insecure ego through possessions or achievement as natural and worthwhile, no one questions the insecure ego itself. That is more or less taken for granted, as the nature of things, as the way it is with everybody.

Contrast this with the practice and effort of keeping something to yourself, holding the experience within and having an inner dialogue with it. To do this in the face of social pressure to flaunt your worth, proclaim your achievements and fatten your CV, calls for virtues that are not so much in vogue—integrity, honesty, humility, authenticity and discipline. The rewards for inner work are inner, not necessarily 'outer'. And we intuitively understand the common wisdom that what is most precious must be guarded the most closely.

Come into my eyes, my love
I will shut my lids and hide you
I won't see anyone else
Nor let you see another
—Kabir

Several songs in the tradition urge us not to give our heart's secrets away to just anybody.

Don't spread your jewels
In a rowdy fish market
Quietly tie your bundle
And be on your way

Jesus puts it rather strongly in the New Testament when he says: 'Do not give what is holy to dogs, and do not throw your pearls before swine, or they will trample them under their feet, and turn and tear you to pieces.'

The nirgun meditative tradition strongly advises the seeker not to disperse the guru's words casually. The mantra or name or word given by the guru cannot be shared.

Once when I was sharing one of these songs in an orphanage in Kolkata, I asked the children why one's love for Shyam, or Krishna, must be kept secret, as suggested in the song:

For a few days, deep in your heart
In a corner of your body-house
Keep your love for Shyam secret!

They proposed an answer which seemed entirely obvious and natural to them. One boy responded in this way: We must keep this love secret because the moment we start talking about it, we become more interested in talking than in love! We substitute tales of Krishna for Krishna.

Even a deeply authentic experience can lose its meaning and capacity to transform if it becomes fodder for display and self-aggrandizement. These are treacherous waters for the self-seeking personality. And perhaps that is why we are later advised quirkily in that same song to bathe in the river of Shyam, but not let our clothes get wet!

For a Few Days

For a few days, deep in your heart
In a corner of your body-house
Keep your love for Shyam secret!
Speak in hints in the pastures of love
Let no one guess
No one hear, no one understand!

When Shyam's memory troubles your heart
Look at the dark clouds in the sky
Hide the tears that well up in your eyes
Put wet wood in the stove for smoke
For a few days...

Go bathe in the river of Shyam
But don't let your clothes get wet!
Swim to your heart's content but beware
Why should your clothes get wet?
For a few days...

If you're headed north, be alert
Tell everyone you're going south!
Lovers delight in this wine's secret
What will a dry heart understand?
For a few days...

—Roshik Das; Bengal

Don't Make a Big Fuss

Stay quiet, don't make a big fuss
Meet a hundred sinners
But stay away from the fool
At the shrine of saints
Meet with ancient seekers

Get the guru's wealth with stealth
Don't make an exhibition
You will kill your own practice
If you broadcast it casually
Stay quiet, don't make a big fuss

Churn the pot of gems and pearls
But don't try to garner butter
If you do, clarify it on the fire
It'll stay free of impurity
Stay quiet, don't make a big fuss

The rohida flower looks lovely
But don't pluck it off the tree
If you do, you'll see its futility
There is no fragrance in it
Stay quiet, don't make a big fuss

Countless rivers flow before you
Don't go jumping into each
If you do, you're sure to drown
Only true seekers swim across
Stay quiet, don't make a big fuss

Come in truth and go in truth
The word of truth alone is truth
Kabir says, listen seekers
The path is solitary and tricky
Stay quiet, don't make a big fuss

—Kabir; Rajasthan

No One Understands My Words

O my friend
I'm an Easterner, from an eastern land
No one understands my words

O friend
Only one who is from the east
Can grasp my meaning
No one shares in my secret
To whom should I open my heart?
Whom should I hold dear?

O friend
A sesame seed is better whole
Or with its oil extracted
A half-ground seed is useless
Neither here nor there
No one understands my secret

O friend
The vine and its leaves are bitter
And bitter is the fruit
But once the true Word is known
The fruit drops off the vine
No one shares in my secret

O friend
The vine has caught fire
And the seed is destroyed
Says Kabir to Dharamdas
No more desire to grow again
No one understands my secret

—Dharamdas; Rajasthan

The Secret of Song

O Seeker, the secret of song is unspeakable
The rare one will grasp it

What do you sing, write and preach
What for this rambling through existence?
What use your evening prayers and rituals
Without contemplating the essence?
The secret of song is unspeakable…

You shave your head, or sport dreadlocks
Or smear ash on your body for the prize
But will bowing down to an idol
Or eating only fruit suffice?
The secret of song is unspeakable…

He who sets up as sage without insight
Gripped by lures of mind and sense
Doesn't penetrate to the heart of wisdom
His speech swells up with arrogance
The secret of song is unspeakable…

Pathless, fathomless, of an untold depth
Where remained neither field nor seed
There the seeker surrendered to the secret
Slashed through the binding pattern of deeds
The secret of song is unspeakable…

Those who feed on inner essence
Those who contemplate the core
Listen to what Kabir says, O Gorakh
They and their kin will reach that shore
The secret of song is unspeakable…

—Kabir; Malwa

It's Between Me and My Lord

O people, what would you know?
It's between me and my god!

Looking for gold? I have none.
Seeking a head? Here I am!
Call me infidel if I turn away from him
It's between me and my lord

O meddlers, what would you know?
It's between me and my god!

Mansoor was hanged for his words
Only the Beloved knew its inner truth
O mullah, perform the last rites!
It's between me and my lord

O busybodies, mind your own business
It's between me and my lord!

I am a seeker of Haider
The true king of kings!
Get me a drink of heaven's nectar
It's between me and my lord

Just do me this small favour
O Keeper of the Faith, Haider
Consummate my life-term
It's between me and my lord

O people, what would you know?
It's between me and my lord

—Bulleshah; Sindh

10. ULAT / UPSIDE-DOWN

It seems to be one of the more exasperating experiences of life that whenever we get into a groove, life brings along a reversal. Just when we begin to get comfortable, thinking that 'things are going well', things begin to go badly. In the old days, people tried to forestall the 'evil eye' of fate through black marks on the skin or demon heads in front of doors or by touching wood. Yet, like waves in the ocean, things are constantly up and down. Fortunes rise and fall. Destiny smiles and subsequently turns her head away. Praise is followed by blame, success by failure. Minds whirl at sudden changes in fortunes.

Or then again, once upon a time it 'made sense' for the woman to stay at home and for the man to go out and earn a living. Or for people to inherit the professions of their fathers, whether kings or shoemakers. Or for everyone to assume that the earth was the centre of the universe and that the sun and entire galaxies revolved around it. Our most fundamental social or cultural assumptions may get overturned in the dramatic sweep of an age. Suddenly nothing makes sense anymore.

Perhaps right now, in this very historical instant, we are in the midst of some assumptions that may be abruptly reversed. That the economies of nations must grow endlessly and that there are no limits to growth. That all experience can be explained in terms of matter, or biochemistry. That nation-states are 'natural' entities. Or, in a more personal space, that we are the centre of somebody's universe—a partner or a child—and this assumption may come crashing down one day. An indiscretion, an infidelity, an accident, a death… and everything changes. The Buddha had it right all along. Whether personal, social or political (or even just physical), there is no escape from change. Love turns to hate. Enemies become friends.

A popular tradition of poems in Kabir and other Bhakti and Baul poetry, variously termed ulatbaansi or sandhyabhasha (upside-down verse or twilight language), insistently turns things on their head. These poems revel in reversals. They defy and mock our conventional notions of truth and how things work. They challenge us to make sense of what seems to be nonsense. They pull the rug of assumptions from under our feet and leave us with no ground to stand on.

O wise one, I was the first to be born
Then my elder brother
With great fanfare my father was born
In the end my mother

They inform us that fish are climbing up on trees, that the rabbit is hunting the lion in the forest, or that there is a whole ocean within a marketplace. They challenge our usual sense of 'knowing', our unquestioned self-assuredness, our safely held beliefs and convictions. Our fearful instinct is to cling to ideas we take as 'truths' in order to make sense of our worlds. These poems scoff at that instinct. They blow our minds with impossible images and scenarios… and then call us idiots for not getting it.

What might be the purpose or point behind such a tradition of poetry in a stream of verse which we understand as mystic? Some say that it is to code a secret knowledge. The images conceal esoteric truths: 'tiger' or 'elephant' stands for 'mind', 'rabbit' for the 'spirit', and so on. Only the initiated may have access.

This is a strangely solemn way to read a verse which is obviously full of delight. Perhaps children understand it best. Because, above all, they delight in it. And then they come up with explanations which are even more bizarre than the poetry itself.

The earth turned into a piece of bread
The crow is flying away with it
Go ask your guru
Now where is he going to sit and eat it!

Unlike the adult, the child has many answers. The crow will go to the moon. No, wait. The crow will go to space. He doesn't need to sit there because there's no gravity! Or, wait. Better still, the crow will go to the sun! But isn't the sun too hot? It's an upside-down world, silly. The sun is quite cool here!

Taking delight along with the poets in this 'nonsense' verse is perhaps the key to accessing a wisdom in lightness, recognizing that things don't only 'make sense' with the mind, that there are other portals to intelligence, especially joy and delight. Also, to be shaken out of our usual ways of seeing is potentially to see something new.

Perhaps there are no real meanings of these songs. Or perhaps they are coded, a kind of cryptic language describing a seeker's experience of various stages of yoga or tantra, which only another seeker can decode. Or perhaps both. Or neither.

Every day we see the world around us. Isn't it a world gone mad? Kabir says this:

Seekers, look, the world has gone mad
If you speak the truth, they beat you up
If you speak falsehoods, they believe you

In such a world, perhaps the only thing that truly makes sense is the one that doesn't seem to make sense. All our 'normal' values are upside-down, from the mystic's point of view. On the other hand, 'they' seem mad to us (that's why, 'mystic'). They tell us to learn to lose, instead of trying to win. They say that renunciation, not acquisition, brings the greatest joy. They tell us not to rise high, but to be the lowest of the low.

And then they speak in these impossible riddles. How can all this make sense to our ordinary minds? *Can* we 'make sense' of this? Or is there an extraordinary truth that these songs hint at, or seek to describe, which only a leap of awareness beyond the logical mind can reach?

Perhaps the answer precedes the question.

Words, These Words

Words, these words of wisdom
Signs of my guru
Birthed in the unmanifest
No wind, no water

Pouring earth
Drenched sky
Water flowing up
From eaves to the ridge!

Traveller walks
Path gets tired
Old woman dozes
Her bright bed snores!

Washerman washes
Washing-stone wrings dry
On top of the clothes
The wet fence dries!

Kabir says this
Listen fellow seekers
The world won't fathom
My unruly words

—Kabir; Malwa

By the Side of the Well

By the side of the well, O seeker
A tamarind tree was planted
Fish have climbed
All over its branches!

Give a nod of greeting for me
To the wandering yogi

By the side of this well
A doe got married
She gave birth
To five baby-deers

The rabbit has turned
Hunter in the forest
He's hunting down
The deer of attachment

The castrated bull gives milk
The cow churns the cream
A rare one tastes
Butter made by this trick

Sheltered in his guru's grace
Gorakh says
Whoever looked for it
Found it

—Gorakhnath; Rajasthan

I Saw Fish Climb up a Tree

I saw fish climb up a tree
A rabbit scare a lion
An ant wrestled with a crane
Who won, who lost?
In your body!

Sinners and swindlers
Rule over this kingdom
Hey look, those who can
In your body!

Wave turned as big as an ocean
The blind man claims he sees!
The naked yogi's clothes are stolen
The lame guy says he can run!
In your body!

Fire says I've got the shivers
Water says I'm thirsty!
Grain says I'm getting hungry
Butter says I'm dry
In your body!

Says Kabir, listen seekers
A rare one found this path
One who searches out this way
Reaches heaven's heart
In your body!

—Kabir; Kutch

Watch This Play, Boy!

Watch this play, boy
Unfolding in your body-fort
Your old fort
Your twisted fort

In this body the five disciples
Yes, o seeker, yes!
Become warriors and fight
Watch this play…

It rains on a clear day
Yes, O seeker, yes!
Lightning and thunder explode
Watch this play…

A steed gallops without any legs
Yes, o seeker, yes!
It sprints on the wind to the sky
Watch this play…

In this body a caged parrot
Yes, o seeker, yes
Trills: 'You're that!', 'You're that!'
Watch this play…

Kabir says, listen up seekers
Yes, o seeker, yes
The bureau of bhakti is abuzz!
Watch this play…

—Kabir; Malwa

The Heart-Secret of This Wandering Heart

The heart-secret of this wandering heart
My guru knows it well!

The ocean runs dry
While waves douse the marketplace
When my father wasn't born yet
My son held his bride in embrace
The heart-secret...

The cow wasn't pregnant yet
When the deal for a plough was sealed
The farmer was still in the womb
When his meal got brought to the field
The heart-secret...

Madan Shah Fakir says
Does it seem all topsy-turvy, friend?
But if you catch the drift of this
Then all your wandering would end
The heart-secret...

—Madan Shah Fakir; Bengal

Time Is Slipping Away

Time is slipping away, my friend
Meditate—time is passing away
Take the path of Raam's name
Quit this silly pride

O wise one, I was the first to be born
Then my elder brother
With great fanfare my father was born
In the end my mother
Time is slipping away...

O wise one, first the yogurt was set
Then the cow got milked
While the cow was yet to deliver
The butter fetched a good price
Time is slipping away...

The ant goes to her husband's home
Nine bags of kohl, her dowry
In one hand, she carries an elephant
Under the other arm, a camel
Time is slipping away...

The unborn child could speak
The newborn child says nothing
Says Kabir, listen seekers
Fools can go on guessing
Time is slipping away...

—Kabir; Rajasthan

My Spinning Wheel Chants the Name of Raam

A drop fell in the ocean
A pearl took shape in water
I heard of such a miracle
A girl gave birth to her father!

Listen to my plea
O listen to my call
My spinning wheel
Chants the name of Raam
It cries, you, only you, only you!

The girl says to her father
Find me an unborn mate
If you can't find me such a partner
Then share my bed and fate!
Listen to my plea…

My wheel is colourful, wonderful
The cotton balls are rosy, red
The one who spins, a pretty young girl
From the sky hangs the thread!
Listen to my plea…

I went to get the cotton ginned
Listen, O cotton-ginner
This ginner got gobbled by his lover
The guru showed me the way
Listen to my plea…

Mother will die, father will die
Husband too is headed for doom
Only the beloved carpenter won't die
The crafter of this loom!
Listen to my plea…

Says Kabir, listen seekers
Listen to the wheel intone
Be the one who spins it well
Then birth and death are gone!
Listen to my plea…

—Kabir; Kutch

11. GURU

India is the unparalleled land of gurus. Perhaps they are our foremost exports. From transcendental meditation to superconscious sex, we have gurus for everything. Especially in modern times, the need for gurus seems to have grown exponentially. Supply cannot keep up with the demand! And so gurus are grabbed hold of as soon as they sprout.

Facetiousness aside, perhaps it would be useful to reflect on this fundamental need for a guru or a teacher, for guidance, for someone to show us the way. On the one hand, as adults we are expected to be in charge, in control of our lives, our minds and wills. On the other hand, we may feel quite lost, confused and clueless about the purpose of life and of our being in the world.

Where do we look for answers? When mid-life crisis hits (sooner and sooner these days), and all our previously held values seem mistaken, where do we turn? It is natural to look to someone who seems to know.

The guru is a very hallowed station in Indian philosophy. There are gurus not only in the sacred sense, but also in more secular domains. For example, the arts. Any classical musician or dancer could speak to you about the importance of the guru in learning and imbibing their art form. But also, since the Indian arts are so closely linked with a sense of the sacred, often the two spaces seem to merge into one. The guru is a powerful figure because he or she has the potential to bring us close to the sacred, which is the highest that a being can aspire to in this life, according to traditional thought.

Only one who has gone before can show you the way. This is the function of the teacher or the guru. To show us the way, our way. But walking remains our task. One fundamental misconception that seems to have accrued around the idea of guru is that s / he can save us, or deliver us, or 'take us across'. No teacher of mathematics can learn the algebra on our behalf. No dance teacher can dance with our bodies. We'll have to do it ourselves.

The guru in the spiritual sense shows us the way to our truest self, or a deeper dimension within us, from which we seem to be disconnected. This is described in poetry by various names: the jewel of Raam's name, the light in the body, the formless, nameless, supreme or invisible, the city of emptiness, the palace of the Word. If s / he can help us get 'there', or put us in touch with 'that', no wonder that the guru is the object of such reverence.

Guru and Govind, both stand before me
To whom should I bow?
I surrender to the guru
Who showed me the path to Govind
—Kabir

On the other hand, it is good to beware of getting attached to figures, personalities or cults. In this sense, Kabir keeps reminding us that ultimately the guru is within. He takes great pains to keep pointing out that there are all kinds of gurus, and that many of them are fake. To distinguish the two, he often resorts to the term 'satguru', or the true guru.

Contrary to modern conceptions, the guru is not a space of 'feeling good', there to massage your ego and relieve you of some of your excess wealth in the process. The guru strikes. The guru lands a fatal blow. She's a hunter, a warrior. In other similes, he's a potter.

The guru's a potter, the disciple a pot
One gives form to the other
The inner hand lends support
The outer hand beats it into shape!
—Kabir

One could say that the guru is a 'tatva', a fundamental element or substance of the universe. It could manifest in a person outside, whom we revere and from whom we learn. It could equally well manifest in our own bodies, and guide us from within. In one poem, Kabir addresses the teacher directly, and reminds him that the prophet or the messenger lies between a person's own eyes. In another couplet he says that the guru belongs to the sky.

Guru in the sky
Disciple in the mind
When awareness merges with the Word
The two are never separated

In this way, Kabir hints often enough that the ultimate guru is the Word—the primordial, unstruck sound, from which all creation comes. All gurus stand in for that guru. And sometimes that guru manifests in one's own body.

One way or another, from without or within, the aim is to be guided and to keep walking, not to pitch camp and set up idols by the side of the path. The true guru asks us for more than that.

In the Sufi tradition, the relationship with the murshid is often ecstatic, bordering on the romantic and erotic, like Rumi with Shams, Amir Khusro with Nizamuddin Aulia, or Bulleshah with Shah Inayat. It is this mad, passionate love for the guru, who is also the beloved, which made Bulleshah train in song and dance for nine months from a professional woman dancer. To win back the favour of his beloved guru, who was upset with him, Bulleshah dressed up like a woman and danced, because he knew his guru was fond of dancing. The relationship with the guru, then, can also be a relationship of mad love, of self-abandon in song and dance.

My True Guru Is Calling

I'm off to fill water from the well
My true guru is calling out to me
I'm on my way!

O my mind!
I leave my childhood home for my beloved's
This house seems too desolate to me
My true guru is calling out to me…

O my heart!
Not a moment's peace without the guru
My immature youth is now behind me
My true guru is calling out to me…

Between earth and sky!
In this vast sky there's an upside-down well
It is overflowing with nectar
My true guru is calling out to me…

Between left and right!
Left and right is the path of misperception
You must walk on the central channel
My true guru is calling out to me…

O my heart!
Sattar Das has found his great guru
He whispers his secrets in my ear
My true guru is calling out to me…

—Sattar Das; Kutch

To Gaze upon My Guru

I will go to gaze upon my guru
I'll bring back the wealth of Raam's name

Body, mind, wealth, all surrendered to the guru
I'll make an offering of my head

I'll light the lamp of the Name in my heart
I will offer up the food of love

All holy places given up to the guru
I will bathe in the Ganges that flows here

Seated in the boat of Raam's name
I will cross the ocean of becoming

Says Kabir, listen seekers
I'll seal the deal for the immortal house

—Kabir; Rajasthan

No Giver Like the Guru

There's no giver like a guru
The world is full of beggars
There's no giver like a guru
No one, o no one!

A boat made of paper
Weighed down with a ton of iron
A true guru can get it across
A saint's words are calling out to you
There's no giver like a guru

Why talk of kings and emperors?
They all stretch out empty hands
The true guru's wisdom extends
In the nine worlds and seven continents
There's no giver like a guru

A criminal takes off for a holy dip
Will holy dips save him?
Stains of deceit don't wash away
Though you scrub ever so hard!
There's no giver like a guru

Says Kabir, what have you lost?
What are you looking for?
O blind one, don't you see
The light is in your own body?
There's no giver like a guru

—Kabir; Malwa

Guru Shatters the Pitch Darkness

Water douses fire, wind dries up water
Each moment a new wave rises
In the temple
Light the lamp and there's radiance

The guru shatters the pitch darkness
The lamp dispels the utter darkness
In the temple
Light the lamp and there's radiance

Such a small bundle
It will bite the dust one day
It will mingle with the mud
In the temple
Light the lamp and there's radiance

The sugarcane stem
Is juicy and sweet
Each knot has a special taste
In the temple
Light the lamp and there's radiance

Begging bowl in hand
You went round the whole town
No one lends oil to a fool
In the temple
Light the lamp and there's radiance

Says Kabir, listen seekers
Dwell upon the formless
Take the name of the nameless
In the temple
Light the lamp and there's radiance

—Kabir; Kutch

The Guru Made the Unknown Known

The guru made the unknown known
That ball of light, that supreme wisdom
He showed me within the body, O brother
The guru made the unseen visible

Mind, intellect, speech can't reach there
Scriptures stutter to speak of it
The indivisible permeates everything
He sang of it as 'Not this, not this'
The heart-guru made the unknown known

Shiva, Sankadik, Brahma wring their hands
As Hari eludes their grasp, O seeker
Vashisht and Vyas couldn't reason it out
No one plumbed its depths, O brother
The true guru made the unseen visible

Like oil in seed, like fire in wood
Like ghee hidden in milk, O seeker
Meaning in word, matter in material
Like melody in the note, O brother
The heart-guru made the unknown known

In the seed is shoot, tree, branch and root
Leaf, flower, fruit and shade, O seeker
So the self contains the Supreme
Being, divinity and all creation, brother
The true guru made the unseen visible

Chants, postures, fasts and prayers
He freed me of this muddle, O seeker
Kabir says, the gracious one gave grace
He showed me my true self, O brother
The heart-guru made the unknown known

—Kabir; Rajasthan

The Prophet Lies Between the Eyes

O teacher, my prophet lies
Between my eyes

Black in white
In the pupil, a star
Unknowable, unseen—
My lord
O teacher…

In the centre of the eye
A bird shimmers
In the bird
A door
On that door
I put a telescope
And navigate this world-ocean
O teacher...

I live in the city of emptiness
A complete one makes it there
Kabir and his lord are together forever
They dwell in the palace of the Word
O teacher...

—Kabir; Urban

The Unbounded Guru

My guru is a merchant
Doing a brisk trade
Without a balance or scales
He weighs the whole world

*

My guru is a warrior
He strikes with the Word
He hurls the bomb of wisdom
And wipes out delusion

*

My guru is on a hunt
Red bow in hand
Idiots escape unharmed
A true seeker is struck down

*

Others strike with guns and cannons
And wound only the body
My guru strikes with the Word
And turns you upside down!

*

Gurus with big beards are bound
A guru beyond bounds is rare
When you meet the boundless guru
Then you find your true place

*

All these are gurus within bounds
Not gurus of the unbound
In the house of experience
The unbounded arises spontaneously

*

'Yes' doesn't quite catch it
'No' is not quite right
In the space between 'yes' and 'no'
My true guru hides

—Kabir; Malwa (set of couplets)

I've Found the True Guru

I've found the true guru
I've found the beloved guru
The chant of 'I am' fills my being
I turn away from frauds and cheats
My mind dwells at the guru's feet

Connect with the golden thread
Drink from the curving channel
Leaving aside both left and right
Remember the central breath
I've found the true guru…

All your nine doors are open
While the tenth is locked shut
Ask your true guru for the key
And open the tenth door
I've found the true guru…

The way across is on the peak
Take the path of the guru's words
A billion suns burst with brilliance
See the lamp and wick there
I've found the true guru…

Those wounded by the word
Stay absorbed, no need to speak
Nanak Das says, listen seekers
One in a million plays this game
I've found the true guru…

—Nanak Das; Malwa

The Guru Gives the Roots

The guru is one who
Gives the roots of wisdom
I love those roots very dearly
Filled with tender nectar

In the body-city, there's a big house
The roots are hidden there secretly

Five snakes, twenty-five she-snakes
Die instantly if they get a whiff of them

The black goddess ate up the whole world
But she trembled on beholding the guru

Kabir says, listen seekers
Cross over with your whole clan

—Kabir; Malwa

Your Love Has Made Me Dance

Your love has made me dance like mad
Come quickly, O healer, or I'll be dead

Your love has built a home in my heart
This cup of poison, I drank of my own accord
O my complete guru, now you must save me
Your love has made me dance…

The sun has set, only redness remains
I'd give my life for just one glimpse of him
I forgot you, O teacher, I let you down
Your love has made me dance…

In the forest of this love, a peacock calls out
My love is more beautiful than any holy place
He wounded me, then forgot all about me
Your love has made me dance…

Bulleshah is called to Shah Inayat's door
He who coloured me in red and green
He who was always lying in wait for me
Your love has made me dance…

—Bulleshah; Punjab

12. THE NAME

Take the name, remember the name, the name will take you across! The poets insist on the importance of the Name. The Name is an entity in itself. It represents sound. It has power and force. It is the doorway to the thing.

Islam speaks of the ninety-nine names of Allah. The whole Sufi practice of dhikr / zikr, or remembrance, is based in part on the repetition of one or several of these names. In the Bhakti space, the Name is an intensely personal thing. Often it is invoked as 'nij naam', your own, personal name. The name is given in strict confidence by the guru to his or her chosen disciple, upon initiation. The disciple then uses this secret name, conferred upon her personally, to do her meditation.

The name itself is not secret—it could be Aum or Raam or Govind or Hari or any other popular name of a deity, or it could be a mantra, that is, a specific combination of syllables charged with energy. But it is secret because it is particular to you. It is meant for you, and you alone. You are not meant to talk about it, to exchange notes with others about it, to broadcast it, to make it common. It gains in power only if you keep it to yourself. This is not in order to hide, but in order to treasure. We can make something our very own only by staying with it over a long period of time and in inner solitude.

Also, the idea is that this particular name or mantra, given to you by your particular guru, is the best vehicle for you to connect with the sacred within. It vibrates to your particular frequency. For another person, it would be another name or a different mantra. One name is not better or more preferable than another name. Different names are simply appropriate for different people.

The proposition is: to remember is to repeat; to repeat is to remember. This is not mechanical repetition, but rather, repeating with remembrance. And, also, remembering to repeat. Forgetful as we are, distracted easily by our daily pursuits and concerns, to remember is indeed a big deal. The Sanskrit word 'smriti' refers at once to remembering as well as awareness. Indeed, in this tradition, the two are one.

The Name is intimately connected with the breath. To 'take the name' is simultaneously to be aware of the breath. To be aware of the breath in each moment—this is the essence of meditation.

On the loom of Raam's name
The warp and weft is the sun itself
Be aware of each rising and falling breath
This is the key to liberation
—Kabir

To remember the Name is one of the foremost tasks enjoined to us by the Bhakti poets. Perhaps this doesn't so much mean that one has to find a guru, get initiation, receive a 'Name' and then begin to chant or remember it. It is perhaps meant as a larger idea of remembrance or awareness at all times. To come back to the body, to connect with that inner sound or frequency which the 'Name' represents, to be with the breath, to recover from the deleterious effects of our everyday distraction and forgetfulness, that is perhaps the deeper meaning of 'remembering the name'.

What we truly love, we remember. The Russian-Armenian mystic, G.I. Gurdjieff, proposed the idea of 'remembering oneself' as the way to ultimate self-knowledge and realization. Perhaps this is the true meaning of loving oneself. The Name represents a sound within. It is not a sound that can be heard with the ears. It is subtle, very subtle. To chant the 'chantless chant' is also to listen.

A seeker
A truly wise one
Listens
There is a sound in the sky
Subtle, so subtle
—Kabir

The 'sky' is the empty space within. To connect with this subtle sound—through a mantra or through the breath—is to connect with oneself. This is self-remembrance.

The Name is not important for its 'meaning'. It is important for the sound, for its vibration, its frequency. When the chattering mind tunes into this frequency, a moment of genuine silence may arise. This is akin to rain over a parched earth.

Clouds gathered, a gentle rain fell
The harvest was plentiful
Pots of cream overflowed
As zikr heals the soul
Body was cleansed of famine's woes
—Shah Latif

Remember the Name

Remember the Name
Chant the Name
The Name will set you free
One who forgets the name
Wanders aimlessly

The deer grazes the crops in the field
When the keeper arrives, it turns and flees
Remember the Name…

Pearls in a blind man's hand don't stay
A fool fritters his diamonds away
Remember the Name…

The misguided man puts his inner cloth on show
And daubs with perfume his musk-scented robe
Remember the Name…

Seek good company if you want to re-form
Dev Dungarpuri says, the Name transforms
Remember the Name…

—Dev Dungarpuri; Kutch

Allah Hu Allah

God, only god
Great-magnificent god

Allah, O Allah
Great-glorious Allah
Remembering your name
What solace it brings to me

Within me and also separate
What can be said about you?
You are lover and also master
What can be said about you?

God, only god
Great-magnificent god
O, the taking of your name
How it reassures me

Your name is Allah
Whatever form you are in
Whatever face you put forth
I am besotted by you
If you are the flame, Friend
Then I'm your moth

You, only you
The Merciful, the Bountiful
Masker of Sin, Ever-Forgiving
Your radiance is everywhere
O Allah!

—Unknown; Sindh

The Eternal Name

My guru gave me the eternal name
No presence like the guru
She dwells in the house of plenty
A place of no lack
Storerooms spilling over with grace
The place of no lack

O great giver, the bright sun erupts
And moon and stars get swept away
So, all these rites and rituals
Are blinded by the light of the name
The guru gives the eternal name

A blaze arose in the ocean's depths
A fire that can't be lit by a hand
Worthless your perusals of holy texts
The name is the way to that land
The guru gives the eternal name

O great giver, a gift like the name
Can't be wasted on an ignorant one
Like an owl knows only star-light
He knows nothing of the sun
The guru gives the eternal name

O great giver, the mind gets unaware
Let us ever remember the name
So, says Kabir, a person may reach
His true abode, from where he came
The guru gives the eternal name

—Kabir; Malwa

Meditate, My Friend

Dwell, dear friend
On Raam, Govind, Hari

Meditate, my friend
On Raam, Govind, Hari

Sing, O friend
Of Raam, Govind, Hari

It doesn't require
Austerities or long practice
No moolah spent
Dwell, dear friend…

Wealth and family
Bring pleasure
But also forgetfulness
Meditate, my friend…

Remember Raam's name
Death hangs like a sword
Over your head
Sing, o friend...

Kabir says, the one without
Raam on his lips
Bites the dust
Dwell, dear friend...

—Kabir; Urban

Raam Chants in My Every Vein

All forests became sacred
All mountains holy
All rivers became like the Ganga
When I found the Raam within

*

Now Raam chants in my every vein
And echoes in every pore
The sound arises spontaneously
This is the essence of meditation

*

I don't turn the rosary beads
Nor take the name of Raam
Now Raam chants my name
And I'm perfectly at ease

*

Raam's name is in abundance
Grab it with both hands, if you can

Or in the end you'll repent
When life ebbs out of you

—Kabir; Malwa (set of couplets)

While You Are Well

Sing the praises of Hari, brother
While you're well and the body is game
You won't remember to do it later
When your frame is rattling with pain

O yes, my fortunes improved, the stream
Merged with the ocean, my true guru came
If you're a swan, then seek
The precious jewel of the Name
Sing the praises...

Meditate while you still have youth
Don't delay, brother, don't wait till the end
A restless old age awaits you
Your heart will lose all patience
Sing the praises...

Life slips through our palms like water
Each moment, each instant, trickling away
The swan returns to the great mountain lake
It won't pass anymore on this way
Sing the praises...

O yes, the god of all gods is Raam
The saint among saints
Kabir says, meditate
And merge into that ocean of bliss
Sing the praises...

—Kabir; Rajasthan

13. OCEAN

The sea is a field of mystery. In this it resembles life, and so it becomes a common theme and metaphor within mystic poetry. Life itself is often described as bhavsaagar, or the ocean of becoming. And we have somehow to cross or navigate this ocean. This needs skill, because the ocean often rocks our boat and throws us about. There are storms and countless other perils. But sometimes we might find a boatman who might show us how to navigate. And this boatman, this sailor, may be a fearsome or strange figure.

This ocean is full of jewels.

Your ocean is filled with jewels
A pearl diver will bring them up
—Kabir

The word for pearl-diver in Hindi is marjeeva, which literally means one who dies and lives again. The pearl-diver plunges to his death, into the depths of the ocean, and when he returns to the surface, it's as if he were born anew. This becomes a powerful spiritual metaphor for Kabir and other poets. To plunge into the depths of oneself, to retrieve a precious but forgotten jewel, is also to plunge to one's death in a sense. And if one manages to return from that place, one is as if born again, or called 'twice-born' or 'dwija' in the Indian spiritual traditions. This is also spoken about as the practice of dying before death.

Taste the waves of the ocean, friend
Pearls aren't found in puddles!
—Gorakhnath

The depth and vastness of the ocean are contrasted with much shallower ways of being, clinging to small and limited identities and notions of self—puddles in which we muck about, often all our lives. If one thinks about the eternal conundrum of whether to be a big fish in a small pond, or a small fish in a vast ocean, the spiritual answer is clear. Go to the ocean—be no fish at all; be like the wave instead.

I said all I had to
Now there is nothing more to say
One stayed, no 'other' remained
Like the wave merges in the ocean
—Kabir

Neither Kabir, nor many of the singers who have sung these songs for centuries, lived by the sea. And yet the ocean is a powerful presence in the human imagination, provoking poetry and a sense of the expanse of life, and of individual human possibility. Man is a sea!

Drop in the ocean
Everyone knows
Ocean in a drop
A rare one knows!
—Kabir

In January of 2017 we met Dhruv Bhatt, who might with some justification be called a contemporary mystic poet. As we travelled with him over a period of a few days, he revealed to us how many of his poems 'come to him' as songs—that is, along with the tune. Lovingly he taught us these songs, in many of which the ocean is a strong presence.

The first song in this section is by him, with an intriguing story behind it. Once Dhruv dada was doing a walking pilgrimage along the coast of his home state of Gujarat in western India. On a hot day, he came across a poor farmer hard at work, sweating away in his small field. Moved, Dhruv dada approached him and asked him how he was doing. Flashing a thousand-watt smile, the farmer looked up at him and said: 'I'm full of joy!' It was an unexpected moment of transformation for Dhruv dada. He reports saying to himself: 'Even I don't have the joy that this man does. How does he have it, in spite of his circumstances? And how could I get it in my head to pity him?' Later this poem came to him as a song.

If, suddenly, I were to come across
Someone on the way
And if they were to ask me
Softly,
'How are you doing today?'
Then I would say,
Nature is so bountiful
And like waves in the ocean
I'm at play!

Herman Melville has long ago spoken of the irresistible call of the sea, in the voice of Ishmael in *Moby Dick*. The sea calls Ishmael, and us, so powerfully because like the moon with the tides it stirs something deep in us. And in this shallowest of ages, depth is what we seek to find and hope to return to.

> Whenever I find myself growing grim about the mouth; whenever it is a damp, drizzly November in my soul; whenever I find myself involuntarily pausing before coffin warehouses, and bringing up the rear of every funeral I meet... then, I account it high time to get to sea as soon as I can... There is nothing surprising in this. If they but knew it, almost all men in their degree, some time or other, cherish very nearly the same feelings towards the ocean with me... Yes, as everyone knows, meditation and water are wedded forever.

I'm at Play

If, suddenly, I were to come across
Someone on the way
And if they were to ask me
Softly,
'How are you doing today?'
Then I would say,
Nature is so bountiful
And like waves in the ocean
I'm at play!

In my torn trouser-pocket hide
Many joyful, dancing waves
Even when alone
I'm in a carnival each day
In a tiny bundle
Which can't even be locked
My treasure is as safe as day
Like waves in the ocean
I'm at play!

Water in the eyes comes and goes
But the moistness within never dries
The shore may keep accounts
Of less and more
The ocean doesn't bother about such scores
The sun may rise and set every day
The sky over me is always the same
Like waves in the ocean
I'm at play!

—Dhruv Bhatt; Gujarat

Your Ocean Is Full of Pearls

Your ocean is full of pearls
Your ocean hides many riches
Only a pearl-diver can bring them up

The land of pearl-divers is strange
Those adrift cannot find it
Those who walk the guru's path
Know the pearl-diver's mind
What will others understand?
Only a pearl-diver...

A pot made of unbaked clay
A whirlpool enticed to come in
False this body, false understandings
You set up a crooked business!
Only a pearl-diver...

Giving up self, you enter the ocean
And fix your full attention on the pearl
So you extract the essence of the gem
Now you cannot leave the ocean
Only a pearl-diver...

Make a careful bargain of each breath
Beat the drum of your own being
Keep track of every subtle breath
Then the Breath of the Beloved will appear
Only a pearl-diver...

O Gulabi Nath, I've found the Consummate One
The guru showed me the path
Bhavani Nath takes refuge in his guru
Now this goodness belongs to the master
Only a pearl-diver...

—Bhavani Nath; Malwa

Your Ocean Is Filled with Jewels

Your ocean is filled with jewels,
a pearl-diver will bring them up
In your body are knots of wisdom,
the lord will untangle them

Your mind is a greedy one
Like a fisherman,
it casts nets of delusion
Your ocean is filled with jewels

In the garden the koel calls
A peacock cries out in the forest
The waves of spring are sweeping in
Your ocean is filled with jewels

The weeds and chaff have burnt away
A festival of spring awaits
Surely my days have taken a turn!
Your ocean is filled with jewels

My guru's wisdom explodes
The coward runs for cover
Hey brave one, stand your ground!
Your ocean is filled with jewels

In the army of Guru Ramanand,
Kabir fights fearlessly
He shoots the arrow of the Word
Your ocean is filled with jewels

—Kabir; Malwa

Taste the Waves of the Ocean

Taste the waves of the ocean, my brother
Pearls aren't found in puddles
O seeker-friend

Why lust for another's wife, O brother
Fleeting, like a lifetime
O seeker-friend

Why fall for a stranger, my brother
Short-lived, like a hay-fire
O seeker-friend

My guru's mare is loaded up, O brother
I've dumped the burden of attachments
The mind lets go of the mind's hungers
O seeker-friend

Says Gorakh, with folded hands, my brother
He's found the timeless land
O seeker-friend

—Gorakhnath; Malwa

My Boat Is Sailing Smoothly

My boat is sailing smoothly
O yes, now my boat is sailing smoothly
Neither rain nor storm can disturb it
A blessed saint has climbed on to it

It has no fear of shallow waters
Nor doubts about the deep
If it capsizes, no harm comes to it
This is a strange spectacle!

It can bear even a mountain's weight
With great ease
The guru has shown me how to navigate
I bow to his wisdom

Kabir says, one who rows without a head
Only he can describe this truth
It's an untellable tale of great benediction
Rare is the sailor who understands it

—Kabir; Urban

14. THE ART OF DYING

Several spiritual traditions and mystics urge us to 'die before our death'. But what does this mean? Why is 'dying before death' paradoxically understood as immortality? Who dies? Who was alive earlier? Who remains alive afterward?

These questions are posed by the mind, but they cannot be answered by the mind. Perhaps because it is the mind itself that needs to die. As long as it questions and investigates, answers and 'makes sense', it remains alive. It stays alive with all its fears, hungers, terrors, desires, anxieties, ideas, concepts, notions and the like. Only physical death is able to destroy this mind, upon which we so painstakingly build our identity.

We live in an age where we acknowledge almost nothing but the mind. God is dead. Religion is outdated. Spirituality is hocus-pocus or at best wishy-washy. The arts are nothing but instruments of commerce, mere commodities in a 'rational' market economy. Only the 'scientific temper', in which the mind dominates, counts. This is as true of the humanities (which aspire to be known as 'social sciences') as it is true of the sciences themselves, and whatever aspires to be publicly respectable discourse. Everything must pass muster at the touchstone of the mind.

How radically counter to our times, then, is the call of the mystics, who exhort us to kill the mind, to go beyond the separate consciousness, the personal identity? This idea is perhaps more heretical today than ever before, in an age which is all about constructing one's unique and individual identity. All our likes and dislikes, our opinions and beliefs, our practices and exchanges, our houses and communities, define who we are. This highly individualized universe is constructed mentally, with physical reality serving as a kind of prop. Ideas prove more powerful than things. We are ready to die for what we 'stand for'—but will we ever die *to* it?

There is a quirky story told by Rumi of an Indian parrot caged in the house of a merchant in Persia. When the merchant is preparing to travel to India on business, the parrot entreats him that if he should run across its fellow parrots anywhere, he should tell them of its woes of being caged in a foreign land. When he is on his journey, deep in a jungle, the merchant makes a brief halt. He spies two parrots on a tree and remembers his promise to his own parrot. When he tells these parrots of his parrot's grief, the two parrots flutter their wings frantically and flop dead. Finding this rather strange, the merchant moves on. When he returns home to Persia, his parrot eagerly asks him if he delivered its message, and if he received a reply in return. The merchant recalls the incident in the jungle and tells the parrot that its brother parrots died of grief upon hearing of its woes. To his utter shock, his parrot too flutters its wings and flops dead. The merchant is struck by wonder and amazement at their mutual sympathy. But, after all, he is stuck with a dead parrot. He takes the parrot's body out of the cage and throws it into the street. The 'dead' parrot immediately comes alive and flies away!

The parrot in the cage understood its fellow parrots' message.

There is a kind of vague belief, or indeed terror, that to die to the mind is to die to all of oneself. This may be because we have never experienced anything other than the mind. So one baulks at the very idea of 'dying to the mind'. If all one knows is the cage, then one clings to the cage.

But if the mind is not all there is, if the mind is not the whole of who we are, then we can perhaps feel, or sense, or grasp, that we are dying to only a part of ourselves. There is something else, an awareness, an intense consciousness, an illumination, which stays alive and, indeed, becomes brighter at the dying of the mind. To die in this sense is not to lose oneself but, really, to find oneself.

Sufis denote this dying by the word 'fanaa', annihilation or oblivion. This idea is hard to take in, if one has not had a palpable experience of something other than the mind.

Forget what is past
Start right away
Die today, yogi
Tomorrow everyone will
—Shah Latif

This dying might mean to die to one's most cherished ideas and beliefs, one's most strongly held opinions, one's most desperately important relationships, one's most beloved possessions. Not necessarily 'giving them up', but dying to them internally.

The gallows are the bedroom
Of true lovers
To turn back or hesitate is a shame
Their love belongs to open fields
The vow to embrace death
Is a sign of true lovers
—Shah Latif

Who in their right mind would want this?

In small ways, maybe *we* do. We die to our pasts in small ways and move on. Like a snake sheds its skin when it is time. We die to our older selves in order to grow towards how we would like to be. We give up some of our most precious beliefs as time goes by. We make efforts to die to our smallness, our greed, our anger, our envy, or whatever else bedevils us. We struggle to die to old, worn-out relationships and ways of being. We're trying to die all the time. What a pity that we do not quite succeed!

The yogis or Sufis or fakirs attempt to die completely. In return for this total obliteration of personality, perhaps they gain a certain freedom. Freedom from the million painful deaths we die every day, when we are dragged unwillingly to countless graves, to bury expired relationships, assets or ideas.

Can a dead person be killed again?
Dying before death is deathlessness
—Lalon Fakir

The Beast of the Mind

To which corner of the earth
Will he escape
Who is devoured by the beast
Of his own mind?

Sneaking up, I tighten my grip
In a flash it snaps open the trap
Then the lion roars frighteningly
Assaulting the little bird of the mind

But which beast can bring what harm
To one who can die before his death?
Can a dead person be killed again?
Dying before death is deathlessness

To be dead-alive before one's death
Is to anchor the mind-ship in the guru-ocean
Lalon says my mind's become like a moth
It sees the light and dies inflamed

—Lalon Fakir; Bengal

Birth and Death

You'll be free, o heart, of birth and death
If you practise the art of dying
One who is born dies
One who dies is born again
This birth and death is immense suffering

The sounds of 'A-u-m' are the three Vedas
Dwelling in the root, sacral and navel chakras
One perfected in practice
Knows them with certainty
And loses all craving for sex or wealth

Ida-Pingala, twin energy channels
Chant 'Ham-Sam' with each breath, night and day
Sushumna, the central channel, pierces
The chakras, and sways
At the third-eye, feeling, 'I am that'

Then you hear the surge of the flute
Drums, castanets and cymbals beat
Conches and bells sound without cease
The buzzing of the bee
The tinkling of anklets

On the thousand-petalled lotus
In a joyful ritual
Dance Radha and Krishna
By gopis encircled
If you see this, you will touch
The bliss of love
The direct path to cessation and freedom

—Unknown; Bengal

The Bedroom of True Lovers

I look for the head but can't find the torso
I look for the torso and can't find the head
Hands, wrists and fingers chopped
And dropped who knows where
When oneness is the bride
The groom is cut to pieces

The gallows are the bedroom
Of true lovers
To turn back or hesitate is a shame
Their love belongs to open fields
The vow to embrace death
Is a sign of true lovers

I am wedded to him who
Wields an axe in his hands
In the field of love
No place to hesitate
Let me put my head on the block
Let the beloved drop the blade

—Shah Latif; Kutch (set of couplets)

Village of the Dead

O seekers
Look at this village of the dead!

Sages are dead, prophets are dead
Dead are the living yogis
Kings are dead, dead their subjects
Doctors and patients are dying

Moon is dead, sun is dead
Dead are earth and sky
Bosses of fourteen worlds are dead
What hope of help from them?

Nine are dead, ten are dead
The eighty-eight died easy
Dead, thirty-three thousand gods
Death catches all in its sweep

The nameless Name doesn't die
That's the only truth
Says Kabir, listen seekers
Don't just die wandering!

—Kabir; Varanasi

Births and Deaths Become Easy

A rare one knows the nearing of the end
The highest guru comes in a veil

Remember the unseen, undying one, friend
And births and deaths become easy

There is no rest without residence
Without a resting place, you get robbed
Remember the unseen, undying one, friend

Without the guru, I keep wandering
Without the guru, I circle around
Remember the unseen, undying one, friend

A breath arises from the navel-lotus
Wonderful is your play, O guru
Remember the unseen, undying one, friend

Says Gorakh, hands joined in prayer
Kabir was the perfect seeker
Remember the unseen, undying one, friend

—Gorakhnath; Malwa

15. THE BELOVED'S COUNTRY

Passports and visas, borders and controls, customs and deportations, dominate our age. Immigrants and refugees are looked at with the eye of suspicion in 'foreign lands'. And this is at a time when we are supposed to be living in a global era.

We are bound by the limits of what we identify with—a piece of land, a culture, an economic system. What we seek to protect, or what we aspire to get a piece of.

Kabir and maverick poets of his ilk invite us into another country. This call is not only global, but universal, and also intensely personal. There *are* requirements to enter into this country. There are documents that are needed, forms to fill out, officials to persuade, before you might be granted permission. But they don't even tell us where to apply!

The journey is no easy task either. No airplane or train goes there. No mode of transport suffices. There are no maps. It is a long, long journey. But the guide says that the place is very close!

These poets, these guides, call out towards a land that has no wind and no water, no sun and no moon, no earth and no sky, no birth and no death. It is no country. It is a country.

What might such a land be like? Where is it? In what space? In which time? How may we arrive into the guru's domain?

Perhaps the invitation is to an experience beyond the senses, and even beyond the mind. The mind cannot fathom the fathomless, tongue cannot utter the ineffable, and therefore this experience cannot be spoken of in words. And yet words are used—'not this, not this'—to give us a glimpse of what that 'land' might be like.

A journey into the heart of this country—no country for faint hearts—requires courage. One has to leave all one's usual markers behind and be prepared for nothingness. One has to be a truly intrepid explorer; not a Columbus who is out to colonize and to subjugate, but one who is willing to cross the vast and turbulent oceans of one's own dark self in order to arrive into a land of luminosity, promise and abundance. Not to kill and to plunder, but to be absorbed.

This is reminiscent of certain iconic texts, such as the famous *Heart Sutra* of Buddhism, which describes the experience of 'shoonya':

> Form is empty, emptiness is form… [A]ll things are emptiness … they are not born, they do not cease, they are not defiled, they are not undefiled. They have no increase, they have no decrease. Therefore, Sariputra, in emptiness there is no form, no sensation, no discrimination, no conditioning, and no awareness. There is no eye, no ear, no nose, no tongue, no body, no mind. There is no form, no sound, no smell, no taste, no texture, no phenomenon.[14]

The guru or the beloved or the friend or the neighbour—call 'it' what you will—lives 'there'. We, who cannot think outside boundaries of time and space and mind, how do we understand this timeless, groundless dimension?

Shah Latif makes use of the legend of Umar-Marui to speak of this land. Marui is a beautiful young girl from a pastoral community, the Maroo, who live in a region of the Thar desert called Maleer. She is kidnapped by Umar Soomra, the king of Umarkot. When she refuses to marry him, she's imprisoned in a tower, and plied with threats and temptations by Umar. But she stays unfaltering in her longing for her land, Maleer, and her people, the Maroo. Her longing for her own people and country, based in remembrance, becomes for Shah Latif a figure for the soul's longing for its origins.

This harks back to a creation story based in Islamic mythology. When Allah had finished creating the body of man from the elements, he invited the 'rooh', the soul, to inhabit this new home. Rooh came down from the heavens to check out her new abode. But she found it dark, dank and depressing. She refused to live in this mud puppet made by god. Allah, understanding her difficulty, took a piece of his own radiance, a noor ka tukda, and infused it into the puppet. He then asked Rooh to look again. When Rooh came back to the body of man, she found it much improved, and consented to live there.

When the time came for all the souls of the world to sally forth and live on earth in the bodies of men and women, in their own appointed times, Allah called them all together and addressed the gathering. He asked them to make a promise before they went forth into this new country on their wonderful adventure. 'Tell me,' he said, 'who is your true beloved?'

'You, only you!' replied the souls in unison. Then Allah extracted a promise from them to remember this, even when they are on earth, distracted by the mind and the senses.

Needless to say, the souls forget. But for the odd soul who remembers, she finds herself in a foreign land. She remembers her true beloved, and where she came from, and all her companions there. She longs to return to her own country.

How do we understand these two spaces, the home and the foreign land? Where the hearts rests—that is home. Where the heart is ill at ease—that is a foreign land. For one who has a faint stirring of remembrance, homesickness grips the heart. You realize that the beloved's country is your own place, where you are most at ease. And then this call, this whisper, this secret longing, never leaves your heart, like an emigrant that can never forget his home.

The beloved keeps calling.

Let's Go, My Sweet

Let's go, my sweet
to the guru's country
the beloved's land

Where nothing arises
and nothing subsides
even wind does not enter
Let's go!

I awoke
in this palace of dreams
and I wept
Let's go!

I realized I was asleep
in this palace of dreams
and I wept
Let's go!

I've taken on
the ascetic's robes
I've dyed my cloth saffron
Let's go!

I've left my mother's home
my husband
the company of my friends
Let's go!

Kabir says
to Dharamdas
what a beautiful, crazy game!
Let's go!

—Dharamdas; Kutch

The Country of the Sky

O my awareness
Let's go to the country of the sky!

Kings don't reach there
Nor their subjects
No emperor or master comes near
O my awareness...

Death doesn't reach there
Nor the web of time
No sorrow or distress comes near
O my awareness...

Brahma doesn't reach there
Nor does Vishnu
Serpent-bearing Shiva cannot enter
O my awareness...

Ladu Nath says, listen Kisna
It's a whole, unfragmented space
O my awareness...

—Ladu Nath; Rajasthan

Such Amazing Signs

My true guru showed me
Amazing signs
Such that cannot be told!

In my land
No earth, no sky
Neither wind nor water
Such amazing signs...

In my land
No sun, no moon
Nor nine billion stars
Such amazing signs…

In my land
Neither Brahma nor Vishnu
Nor any god named Shiva
Such amazing signs…

In my land
No Veda, no Gita
No song or couplet either
Such amazing signs…

In my land
No rising or setting
No birth or death
Such amazing signs…

Step by step
A saint made it there
Kabir climbed to liberation
Such amazing signs…

—Kabir; Rajasthan

Such Is My Country

With the secret you can see it
Such is my country

Scriptures didn't fathom it
Nor words and speeches
Beyond eight centres and ten doors
My consciousness reaches
Such is my country…

No clouds yet lightning flashes
Sky lights up without a sun
Pearls are strung without eyes
From the truth arises the Word
Such is my country...

Drums resound in the emptiness-dome
Horns, sitars and sarangis
Climb to the steep sky-cavern, seeker
And behold the peerless-pathless
Such is my country...

Water merged in water
Neither sweet nor saline
Kabir says, listen seekers
With the guru's grace, you arrive
Such is my country...

—Kabir; Malwa

This Alien Country

It's not for me
This alien country
This crazy country

Can't stay anymore
In this barren country

This world is a ball of paper
A splash of water, and it crumbles
It's not for me...

This world is a thorny creeper
It tangles and pricks to death
It's not for me...

This world is a pile of hay
Just one spark, and it burns
It's not for me...

Kabir says, listen seekers
In the end, we have to go
It's not for me...

—Kabir; Rajasthan

City of Mirrors

A city of mirrors jostles my house
My neighbour lives there
I keep feeling: I've seen him, I've seen him
But he's not to be seen
My neighbour lives there

Fathomless water encircles the village
On this bank, neither boat nor boatman
How will you get across?
I see fear in you
My neighbour lives there

What description do I give of this neighbour?
Neither hands nor feet, neither head nor torso
Sometimes dwelling in the void
Sometimes floating on the water
My neighbour lives there

If that neighbour would touch me once
The torments of hell would disappear
That's how Siraj and Lalon are together
At a distance of a thousand miles
My neighbour lives there

—Lalon Fakir; Bengal

My Country's Boundless

I don't know the man
Who knows only the bound
I dwell beyond all measure
O seeker, my country's boundless

Earth is bound, sky is bound
Bound are wind and water
O brother, my country's boundless

Moon is bound, sun is bound
Bound, the nine billion stars
O seeker, my country's boundless

Good guys are bound, bad guys are bound*
All the gods are bound too
O brother, my country's boundless

Shiva is bound, Shakti is bound**
Bound, all there is in the world
O seeker, my country's boundless

Gorakh says, with Machhinder's grace
Inhabit a realm subtler than the bound
O brother, my country's boundless

—Gorakhnath; Rajasthan

*Literally, Pandavas and Kauravas, the opposing forces in the Mahabharata. But the point seems to be larger, and not restricted to a particular story.

**Shiva and Shakti, male and female principles, can roughly be translated as consciousness and manifestation.

Someone from My Land

O, to meet someone from my land
And have a few words with him
To meet but not to speak
Such an old kinship

This wood, that wood, they're all one
The same master made them all
This wood burns in a sacred fire
That one's studded in a palace wall
O, to meet…

This stone, that stone, they're all one
That master fabricated them both
This stone becomes part of the idol
That one's on the temple floor
O, to meet…

Mother earth, the firewood stove
The sky made into a cauldron
All four ages tossed to the flames
The smoke rises to the heavens
O, to meet…

Gorakh folds his hands in prayer
He's found his place in heaven
One who meditates on the true name
Arrives at the true destination
O, to meet…

—Gorakhnath; Malwa

It Rained Last Night

It rained last night
Lightning flickered
Over the land of my kin
It rained last night…

The dark sky thundered
Clouds unclenched their drops
It rained last night…

It poured in Maleer
Green grass shot up everywhere
It rained last night…

Cucumbers ripened in the fields
Creepers ran riot
It rained last night…

The Maroo herded the cattle home
Their huts are where the grass grows
It rained last night…

I've longed and yearned for them
I've suffered a thousand sorrows
It rained last night…

Shah Latif says, listen friends
I beheld my kin in a vision at dawn
It rained last night…

—Shah Latif; Kutch

Lightning Strikes

Destiny captivated me
Why else would I be here?
Fate brought me to this place
But heart, body, breath
Belong to them
O King, let Marui return
To her people!

These are ever festering wounds
I yearn for union
Separation has destroyed me
King, my memory dwells on them
Who dwell in the desert
My eyes thirst for
The sight of my people

Such a fine needle
Knits my heart to my Maroo
An unbreakable bond!
My brittle body and bones
Are with you, king
But my heart's in the desert

Lightning strikes, Umar
It makes me sad
Rain is falling at home, I see
Flashes of lightning
Crown my Maleer like a groom

I see a dream, Soomra
I am in my own country
Passing around sweet berries
From the fruit trees
Herding goat kids
With a stick in my hand

I see a dream, Soomra
I am going home
Plucking fruit with my people
Off the trees on the sand dunes

A new day dawns, I lift my veil
And beseech Allah
Master, reunite me
With the Maroo of Maleer
My heart aches deeply
For my people

I thank those beautiful days in jail
Trapped in my tower I wept
Endlessly, out of longing
Tears of remembrance washed away
My earthly desires
Love released me from the illusory
Shackles of captivity

—Shah Latif; Kutch (set of couplets)

16. SONGS OF FULFILMENT

It's remarkable how little we seem to love ourselves; how little joy permeates our life. Would we say that we are truly content and satisfied? What would we say about our state of being if we were to be brutally honest? What would we say about those around us?

Expressions of deep fulfilment and bliss in this poetry remind us of what is possible. To sing, to dance, to take in all the fragrances of the garden without being tortured by one's own desire to consume, to not be acting from a deep, fundamental conviction of lack, but rather from a sense of completeness—these are experiences that are perhaps not so close or common to us.

Having been through songs of search, songs of longing, songs of despair, we arrive into the songs of fulfilment. The state of the mystic is inexpressible in ordinary terms. But poetry and song come close to giving some kind of form or expression to this inexpressibility. The poets seem to speak out of a state of elation, joy, exuberance, ecstatic bliss, and sense of arrival, which convinces us that our transient experiences of 'happiness' do not really compare to this. These folks are talking about something else. These guys are on another trip!

The entire universe sings and dances with them when they are on this high. This joy cannot be contained. A larger self explodes into its own consciousness, and ecstatically celebrates itself.

A million suns and moons
Bow down to my beauty

What kind of state is this? It seems something hard to fathom or imagine. And yet we feel a stirring of truth behind it. Such joy is possible!

There are other ways in which the feeling of fullness is expressed. The fullness of a pot brimming over. The fullness of the seeker swimming in the words of truth, this poetry itself! Or the heart-mind that has become a dancer, exuberantly expressing itself in motion.

It is the fullness of meeting and experiencing one's own self for the very first time. This self is full of beauty. And yet this self is not 'I'—make of that what you will.

In some songs this is described in terms of a wedding: the union of the individual awareness (bride) with the universal one (groom). When this union takes place, strange wonders unfold.

The mute have started to sing
The deaf one can listen
The lame guy dances
The blind guy sees!

And who is this blind, deaf, dumb and lame person, if not each of us, carrying around our sense of being incomplete, not seeing, not hearing, not really speaking, never really dancing? We don't see. If only we could see!

Do we even see ourselves? Who are we actually? Mere accidents of evolution? Mere biochemical contraptions? Can all this give joy?

These questions are fundamental and existential. While modern scientists try to decode genetic and / or biochemical patterns to explain the arising of happiness, the mystics have swallowed it, experienced it, and located it within the self. This self is utterly other.

Achal Ram is now himself
The beloved and I are not apart
Suffused with my own radiance
I've merged into my own self

The 'I', the mind, the ego, is riddled with a sense of lack or inadequacy. We watch the rising and falling levels of our usual sense of 'self', measuring and weighing nervously, comparing and evaluating ourselves vis-à-vis others, constantly jockeying for position in the game of life. We win, we lose. We are ahead, we are behind. We are happy, we are miserable. It is all up and down like the waves of the sea.

At the bottom of the ocean, in deep stillness, lies a pearl. The bartender stops serving wine to others, and starts getting drunk herself. When the cup overflows, everything changes. Nothing more to say.

Feeling small, you climbed the scale
You're full now, what's there to weigh?

My awareness, the bartender, has got drunk
Her own wine is making her sway!

I'm drunk on joy
What can I say?

Words of Truth

Words of truth
Fill the seeker to the brim
They seep into her every pore, O yes!

Drink fearlessly, seeker
From the cup of the Name
I've found my true guru today
Awareness climbs to the sky!
Drink fearlessly, seeker

In a whirling cave, my master sits
Hum and find him out, O bee
Strike an inward-looking posture
Get filled to the brim, O yes!
Drink fearlessly, seeker

Lightning flashes on a cloudless day
Boundless light showers, O yes!
Drink fearlessly, seeker

No spear or sword, yet Kheem wages war
My guru Bhaan has whispered the secret
Drink fearlessly, seeker

—Kheem Saheb; Kutch

Soak up the Sky-Nectar

Soak up the sky-nectar, friend
It's raining bliss!

Thirsty for a drop, you drank a whole pot
But dream-water did not appease
How and to whom do I explain this?
A single drop is all one needs
It's raining bliss

Why gulp water without real thirst
This water is for one who seeks
You've got to earn the right to this learning
Then the nectar rains down in sheets
It's raining bliss

Drink this wine to reach eternity
Free from the ache of becoming
No more grief of death or attachment
The body-pitcher fills to brimming
It's raining bliss

The guru's words are drops of nectar
This water is the way of life
Singing with Kabir the branches
Of love remain green and ripe
It's raining bliss

—Kabir; Malwa

My Heart's on Its Feet

My heart's on its feet
It's become a dancer!
Night and day, day and night
The drums of wisdom beat!

The sound has everyone tuned in
Even planets and stars are swinging
There is joy in the city of death
My heart's on its feet!

Clinging to name and status
People try to be special!
With a thousand graces
My heart dances
Wooing the creator
My heart's on its feet!

Thrown in the world-ocean
Swim with the skill of stillness
Kabir says, listen seeker
Become a real disciple
My heart's on its feet!

—Kabir; Urban

My Mind Has Taken to Living Free

O friend, my mind has taken
to living free!

The joy of mindful awareness
Cannot be found in luxury

My mind rejoices in poverty
My heart rejoices in simplicity
My mind has taken to living free!

A bowl and a staff is all I carry
Yet my kingdom stretches wherever I see
My heart has taken to living free!

Praise or abuse, listen to it all
But don't stray from simplicity
My mind rejoices in poverty!

My dwelling in the city of love
Became beautiful with patience
My mind has taken to living free!

Your body will bite the dust one day
Why strut about, so smug, so vain?
My heart has taken to living free!

Says Kabir, listen seekers
The lord is found in contentment
My mind has taken to living free!

—Kabir; Malwa, Kutch

I'm Drunk on Joy

I'm drunk on joy
What can I say?

You found a gem, tied it in your bundle
Why keep opening it for display?
My heart is overjoyed
There's nothing more to say

Feeling small, you climbed the scale
You're full now, what's there to weigh?
My mind is intoxicated
What's left to say?

My awareness, the bartender, has got drunk
Her own wine is making her sway!
I'm drunk on joy
What can I say?

The swan bathes in the great mind-lake
In puddles and ponds, why do you play?
My mind is intoxicated
What's left to say?

Kabir says, listen seekers
I found god in a piece of grain!
My heart is overjoyed
There's nothing more to say

—Kabir; Malwa

Sweep the Path Clear

I sweep the path clear
I strew it with flowers
I've got a glimpse of my Hari

I turned into a cuckoo
And sat in the cloud
I took delight in the thunder

I turned into a bee
And settled on the flowers
I drank in the fragrance

I turned into a koel
And sat in the garden
I basked in all its scents

Meerabai says
By singing Hari's praises
I submitted to his presence

—Meera; Rajasthan

Crow, Sing Sweetly

Crow, sing sweetly of this bliss
Meera's mind is wedded to Raam
It has become his

Beloved, your path is arduous
You spear me with love's sword
Sing sweetly...

Beloved, I walk into your field
And fill my basket with flowers
Sing sweetly...

Beloved, gaze fixed on your face
I wash it each dawn with love's rays
Sing sweetly...

Like a dead leaf turns to gold
Meera is the turmeric-paste you put on
Sing sweetly...

Meera sings your praises, beloved
You've made my heart your own home
Sing sweetly...

—Meera; Rajasthan

No Sun, No Moon

No sun, no moon
Yet there was light
Don't go to other worlds
What you seek is right here!

My dear girl
The mute have started to sing
The deaf one can listen
The lame guy dances
The blind guy sees!
No sun, no moon…

O my friend
Inside the sky-dome
A drunken yogi meditates
There's no holy fire, nor ash
And there is no meditator
No moon, no sun…

My dear girl
On the peak of emptiness
A pitched battle rages
No place for cowards here
They have run for cover
No sun, no moon…

O my friend
Gulabi Das sings
The locks on my heart have sprung open
Bhavani Nath declares
My body is bathed in light!
No moon, no sun…

—Bhavani Nath; Malwa

In This Body

In this body, endless gardens
And the creator of gardens, in this body
But you search in the dark!

In this body, the seven oceans
And the nine billion stars, in this body
But you search in the dark!

In this body, treasures and jewels
And the knower of riches, in this body
But you search in the dark!

In this body, the sound of the universe
And fountains of elation, in this body
But you search in the dark!

Kabir says, listen seekers
My guru, too, is in this body
But you search in the dark!

—Kabir; Urban

Sun-Gourd, Moon-String

Sun, the gourd
Moon, the string
The instrument's stem
An unstruck sound
Tuned to the central energy channel

Play this one-stringed instrument
The string of nothingness
Vibrates subtly, but full of bliss
Sun, the gourd...

Left and right channels interlace
Everybody listens
All tastes become one
Poised, alert in transition time
Sun, the gourd...

The elephant of the intellect
Dances atop the senses
The sound of thirty-two strings
Spreads in all spaces
The goddess sings, plays
And dances
The curtains fall
On the Buddha's great drama
Sun, the gourd...

—Binapad; Bengal

O, She Really Wooed Him

What a groom she found, that crazy girl!
She really wooed him, the darling girl
My awareness has become a bride today
She's taken the lord as husband

Wandering through endless lifetimes
Today the chance has come
If you blow this moment
You'll never find your ground
O, she really wooed him…

They anoint her with the paste of love
The turmeric of awareness
The oil of the Name
Five friends sing songs of celebration
The canopy is decorated with gems
O, she really wooed him…

Truth consecrates the four corners
The groom brings presents of love
Their hands join in an everlasting bond
This union is with divinity itself
O, she really wooed him…

In my colourful palace
Is the bed of my lord
I deck myself in full awareness
Now my love is only for him
All saints join in this grace
O, she really wooed him…

Spinning through endless births
The self marries and comes home at last
Say Kabir, listen seekers—
The swan sings the song of union!
O, she really wooed him…

—Kabir; Malwa

From the House of Farid

From the house of that sugar-trove, Baba Farid
Gesu Daraz has set out as a groom*
All homes wake to songs of celebration
As the moon walks out amid the stars

Look at all who grace the wedding party
Mars, earth, space, lamp, flame
Hazrat Ali brings the groom's headdress
Further down you see Moinuddin Chishti

Ganjbaksh Hajveri stands smiling
Saint among saints, Geelani, is arriving
Shams and Rumi together have come
It's a night heady with song

The wandering yogi Kabir is here
Castanets and drums resound
King and fakir, Nanak appears
All things echo the primal sound

—Madan Gopal Singh; Urban

---

*Poet and singer Madan Gopal Singh composed this song as the imagined wedding of Gezu Daraz, a Sufi saint of the Chishti order—popularly known as Bande Nawaz—whose dargah in Gulbarga in Karnataka had been under dispute. Madan ji explains the context of the song in his own words:

> 'At some point when Uma Bharti was Chief Minister of Madhya Pradesh, she had made a call to Hindus to join her on a protest march to Gulbarga, as part of a wider right-wing movement to destroy the dargah of Gesu Daraz, claimed to be the site of an earlier temple. I created this song which describes the wedding of Gesu Daraz, and arriving at this wedding to bless him are all the ancestors of Sufi and Bhakti lineage! I wanted to evoke the resonances and solidarity between a long and wide history of mystics, Bhakti poets and Sufis, some who passed away centuries ago, some yet to be born.'

I Have Given Up My Self

I am in surrender
I have given up my self
My true guru has come home
I surrender my self

The true guru has come home
I dip into this holy river
My body becomes pure
I surrender my self

Come, friends, let's gather
And anoint him with saffron
Let deep love be our welcome
I have given up my self

The true guru appears
It's a great benediction
He robs me of my illusions
I surrender my self

This company transforms me
I sing songs of praise
My heart-window opens
I have given up my self

Narayan Das sings your glory
And lays his head at your feet
The true guru will guide me
I surrender my self

—Narayan Das; Rajasthan

17. SONGS OF PRAISE

To praise is the whole thing! A man who can praise
comes toward us like ore out of the silences
of rock. His heart, that dies, presses out
for others a wine that is fresh forever.
(Rainer Maria Rilke, 7th Sonnet to Orpheus,
translated by Robert Bly)

In the ecstasy of wonder and fullness, there is perhaps no other expression possible but to render praise. There is not even anything really to say. But speak we must, because to praise enriches us. It brings our own wonder back to ourselves, and deepens the mystery. To praise is to participate in something vaster and deeper than oneself.

It is also to give a name to things, to honour and preserve them in memory, language or the ether, a unique purpose to which human beings seem to be called. The human being can name. To name is to sing praise. That's why there are the ninety-nine names of Allah or the thousand names of Vishnu.

Every now and then, free of ourselves, the sheer beauty of some part of creation strikes us. It takes our breath away. We might wonder: why all this beauty, this decoration, this magnificence? Confronted with grandeur, left with no answers to our paltry questions, wonder stills the tongue for a moment. But then, inevitably, praise erupts. Praise for what, for whom? Praise not for things, or someone, but as celebration, as joy, as festival. An outpouring.

When the mind passes its measure, it either descends into silence or rises into acclamation. In our modern era, we have learnt all too well to analyze. To analyze is to break down, to take apart, to deconstruct. But what about the mind which puts it all together? Is there a measure of that mind? Could we possibly have forgotten the art of synthesis, lost as we are in the throes of the science of analysis?

Unlike us clever modernists, these poets are not afraid to take the name of god. They see that force, whatever it is, manifest in nature, in the human being, in the endless play of variety and form.

You're the brewery, you the bar
You're the bartender
You drink and get others drunk
You're the drunk gone under
—Sachal Sarmast

If everything is the play of that One, to say anything would be redundant. And yet, redundant as it is, poetry is what redeems us. The poet is the one who allows her heart to receive the great feelings of which it is capable. The poet is the one who 'purifies the dialect of the tribe', and expresses its thanksgiving for life, for creation, for community, for well-being. The poet makes an offering, like the poor woman who brings flowers daily for the feet of her stone god.

The one who sings praise goes beyond self. This is the whole idea of bhajan, kirtan, chant.

Taking your name, I merged into you
No 'I' remained in 'me'
I sacrificed myself at the altar
Now wherever I look, I see you
—Kabir

The poet survives in our world of mechanical hardness in order to give praise. It's a wonder that the world survives, and it's a wonder that the poet survives. Rilke, that great poet of praising, speaks of how the earth wishes to speak to herself through us, how the world longs to taste its own delights through our acts and words.

Could we be here, then,
in order to say
House
Bridge
Fountain
Gate
Pitcher
Apple tree
Window
...
Here is the time for telling. Here is its home.
Speak and make known: more and more
the things we could experience
are lost to us, replaced
by mindless doing.
...
Praise the world to the angel: leave the unsayable aside...
[S]how him what is ordinary, what has been
shaped from generation to generation, shaped by hand and eye.
Tell him of things.[15]

Praise, O Creator

Praise, O Creator, to your creation
This painting has no parallel, no frame

All forms depend on you
Yet you are formless
Not subject to birth and death
Beyond form, and boundless
Praise, O Creator...

The breadth of your play is amazing
A rare one penetrates
You appear only to those
Who dwell always in your grace
Praise, O Creator...

Diligently they meditate on you
Saints, seers, ascetics, holy men
In the four directions and endless births
Only you are in evidence
Praise, O Creator...

Your radiance sparkles on every leaf
Like lightning lights up space
Mind and intellect both bewildered
Jeevadas sings your praise
Praise, O Creator...

—Jeevadas; Malwa

No Measure of Your Greatness

There's no measure
Of your greatness
You made this beautiful form
Allah came to earth as man
The lord took birth as human

I'm neither engaged nor married
Yet a child plays in my lap
With the pretext of the forbidden fruit
I exiled myself from Eden
There's no measure…

Cain and Abel are sons of Adam
But who gave birth to Adam?
I was here before Adam was born
I gave birth to Adam
There's no measure…

The magician conjured a trick
And fashioned this puppet
Who plays drums from street to street
Dancing to love's beat
There's no measure…

Mohammad, the veil, Ali, the cloth
The face behind it is secret
My name used to be Ali Raza
Now I'm 'Bulleya', the one who forgot*
There's no measure…

—Bulleshah; Sindh

---

*Bulleshah makes a pun on 'Bulleya' (his own name) and 'Bhoola' (the one who forgot his own name).

You Are My Love

You, just you
O lord
You, just you
O you, you, you
Just you

The heart receives you with joy
But understanding staggers
Now I've understood
This is how to recognize you!

You are my love and my lover
My religion and my faith
My Qaaba and Qibla, mosque and minaret
My holy book, my Qur'an
I've come to recognize you

You are my body and my soul
The core of my being, my life
You are my worry, my meditation
My relish, my ecstasy
I've come to recognize you

You, just you
You are my love and my lover
Just you
Only you

—Khwaja Ghulam Farid; Sindh

Dancing to His Tune

The Beloved's taken the human form
He's got me dancing to his tune!
Look, my beloved's in the human form
How he twirls me around!

You frolic in your own lap
In the form of child Krishna
You sow the seed and water the crops
And are the keeper of the field

You're the brewery, you the bar
You're the bartender
You drink and get others drunk
You're the drunk gone under

Abel and Cain were sons of Adam
Who was Adam the son of?
Tell me, who was Adam the son of?
You threw Abraham into the fire
And yourself raised a hue and cry

—Sachal Sarmast; Sindh

18. ISHQ / LOVE

And finally we arrive at that most mysterious entity of all: love. Dare we even take its name? For the mystic, it is the highest station, the greatest calling, the master key, the philosopher's stone, the thing that describes everything.

Yet love is surely also one of the most abused words in our vocabularies. So perhaps we will let the songs speak for themselves. Amazement, bewilderment, intoxication, unworldliness, reversal, seeing and being seen, being stripped of all pretence, intimacy, union, self-realization, ecstasy.

These poets do not take the name of love lightly, or in vain. Ishq, prem, sneh, preet—these are charged words, denoting everything. Kabir says:

Everyone takes the name of love
But no one understands it
Call that by the name of 'love'
Which has no increase or decrease

That is, it is not dependent on circumstance. This love does not turn into hate. It is autonomous. It flows out, yet it belongs to oneself. It is truly one's own. And yet, it is universal. Kabir says that a person without love is like a dead man walking.

This love is not of the mind. It is not calculated. It is utter, immense, absolute. It is beyond ordinary comprehension.

Hazrat Shah Niyaz says:

Leave behind the school of the intellect
And enter into the tavern of love

I've drunk the drink of death and no-self
Let what will be, will be

All the clichés are true. Love is everything. Love is all there is. Give everything up for love. Love will set us free.

But what kind of love? Allow yourself a taste of the extraordinary state that these ordinary yet remarkable men express in these astonishing songs.

The Tale of Love's Amazement

Hear the tale of love's amazement
No more obsessions, no more fairies
Neither you nor I remained
What remained was this bewilderment

What a strange hour that was
When we learnt directly from love's book
And the book of intellect put aside
Gathered dust on some forgotten shelf
Hear the tale…

A gust of wind from the unmanifest
Scorched the garden of intoxication
Yet one branch of the tree of sorrow—
Let's call it love—stayed alive and green
Hear the tale…

The fire of love turned to ash
The destitute heart of Siraj
No more fear, no more defences
Only a clear fearlessness
Hear the tale…

—Siraj Aurangabadi; Sindh

Drunk on Love

I'm drunk on love
Why be clever anymore?
Free of worldliness
Why play games anymore?

They wander who are lost
Separated from the beloved
My beloved dwells in me
I'm not waiting anymore
I'm drunk on love…

Not once did I lose sight of him
Not once did he leave my side
My heart's strings are tied to him
I'm not restless anymore
I'm drunk on love…

Kabir, get drunk on love
Rid your heart of duality
Such a delicate path to tread
Why carry a burden anymore?
I'm drunk on love…

—Kabir; Urban

My Beloved Has Come Home

My beloved has come home, friends
Get rid of the watchman
That dratted timekeeper!

My love has come home
Allah brought us together
An incredible benediction

Time and again he clangs the bell
And disrupts my night of union
If he understood my heart's desire
He'd toss that clock away!

The limitless melody sounds so sweet
A wonderful singer, rhythm and beat
All ablutions and prayers forgotten
O bartender, hand me the cup of wine!

A glimpse of him is a marvellous thing
It softens all life's stings
May this night never end, do something!
Erect a wall against the morning

Bulleshah's bed is ready and made
I'm in love with the one who saves
This time has come after eons of trying
Now we'll never be parted again!

—Bulleshah; Sindh

The River of Love

Khusro, this night of union
I spent awake with my beloved
This body mine, the mind his
The two became one colour

Khusro, this game of love
I played with my beloved
If I win, he'll be mine
If I lose, I'll belong to him

Khusro says, the river of love
Flows in strange ways
One who escapes, drowns
One who drowns is saved

—Amir Khusro; Rajasthan, Sindh (set of couplets)

Be True to My Love

Be true to my love
Like the poor have no one but their Raam
Be true to my love
Like the weak have nothing but their faith
Don't leave me alone in this life-ocean

You are the tree, I the creeper
I'll stay in your embrace
If you wither, I'll dry up too
What would become of me without you?
Be true to my love…

You are the sea, I the fish
I'll stay immersed in you
If you dry up, I'll die too
What would I be without you?
Be true to my love…

You are the cloud, I the peacock
I'm connected to you
I get great joy from you
When you rain, I sing and dance
What would I be without you?
Be true to my love…

Kabir says, O Dharamdas
The beloved is within your body
The beloved is your own heartbeat
Don't leave me alone in this life-ocean
Be true to my love…

—Dharamdas; Malwa

Love Stripped Me

Once I went to the office of love
Love stripped me of my swagger

I'd gone to garner love's praises
Love robbed me of my vanity

Love swindles saints and prophets
It strips mighty kings of their kingdoms

O naïve Bulleya, what did love steal of yours?
Love looted even god of his godliness!

—Bulleshah; Rajasthan

Come into My Eyes

If my beloved's a red rose
Then I'm his fragrance
And if he's my beating heart
Then I'm his breath

*

O beloved, I belong to your country
But have to live in this foreign land
I do all my work here
But my heart's with you

*

I would write letters to my love
If he loved far away
But what message can I send
To the one in my body, mind, eyes?

*

Come into my eyes, my love
I'll shut them close and hide you
I won't look at anyone else
Nor let you see another

—Kabir; Malwa, Rajasthan (set of couplets)

I Saw Myself

I saw myself
I fell madly in love
Don't mess with me, friends
I'm in ecstasy

A million suns and moons
Bow down to my beauty
Seeing this wondrous form
I blush, what can I say?
I saw myself...

I'm free of the obsession with 'I'
Draped in the shroud of love
My cloth is dyed in all colours
I'm face to face with myself
I saw myself...

Now I behold no one else
In the whole wide world but me
The veil of separation has lifted
All delusion destroyed
I saw myself...

Achal Ram is now himself
The beloved and I are not apart
Suffused with my own radiance
I've merged in my own self
I saw myself...

—Achal Ram; Rajasthan

APPENDICES

SONGS IN ORIGINAL LANGUAGES*

1. GHAR / HOUSE

The Drink of Raam / Raam Ras Meetho Ghano

Main mera ghar jaadiya re, jogiya ji
Liyo paleeta haath
Koi agar jaado ghar aapro re, jogiya ji
Chalo hamaare saath

Raam ras meetho ghano re, jogiya ji
Piye amar hoi jaaye

Ghar jaadyo ghar ubhre re, jogiya ji
Ghar raakhyo ghar jaaye
Ek achambho main dekhiyo re, jogiya ji
Mado kaal ne khaaye

Aage re aage dav jade re, jogiya ji
Peechhe hariya hoye
Balihaari un roonkhdi re, jogiya ji
Jad kaatyo phal hoye

Dhruv piyo, Prahlad piyo re, jogiya ji
Piyo Peepe Ravidas
Bhagat Kabira ras pi rahyo re, jogiya ji
Phir peevan ri aas

~

*The songs are transliterated here into the Roman script in the loose, informal and intuitive style which is the common usage in India. A few couplets of the Sindhi texts are from two books instead of from the oral traditions and transcribed from there. These are: Mani Shankar Dwivedi (trans.) *Shah Latif Ka Kavya* (New Delhi: Sahitya Akademi, 1969) and T.R. Shangari, *Kamil Darvesh: Shah Latif* (Radhasoami Satsang Beas, Dera Baba Jaimal Singh, 2008).

Kaala, My Dark Beloved / Hey Kaala

Hey Kaala hei aamaar
Paagol kori lo re
Aar ghore roi kemone?

Hey Kaala, Kaala
Bole shokhi re
Ae Kaala, ae Kaala, goler maala
Aar ontorete lekha aachhe
Kaala konchon shona roop

Kaala, Kaala!
Bole shokhi re
Kaala, ae Kaala, goler maala
Ontorete jolichhe baati
Kaala jeebon moron re

Shurodhoneer ghaate jaaiya
Shoi aami dekhlaam rooper chhobi
Aar ekaakini jaashe na ghaate
Shokhi aamaar moto hobi re

Kul–o–maan aar jaaye na raakha go

Ki koribo? Kothaaye jaabo shokhi?
Hey aami bhebe na paai dishe re

Bondhur preme ae ki reeti?
Aamaare kul chhaada korilo go

Buker maajhe aamaar tusher onol
Aar jole roiya, roiya go

Aamaar byatha ke boojheebe shokhi?
Ae dil naai shongshaare go

Aar shuno, byatha bethije naai shokhi
Ae bhobo shongshaare

Aar Kaalaar preme moje re shokhi
Aamaar jonom jaaye kaanshia go

Shuno dukhe, dukhe shokhi
Shokhi Raai! Shokhi re!
Kaala aamaar paagol korilo re
Aar ghore roi kemone?

~

One Without a House / Jit Kit Vase Te Tu

Jit kit vase to tu
Aa la-makaan vaalo
Har hand aaye tu
Aa la-makaan vaalo

Chalo to duniya vekhun
Maula Ali pasun
Duniya midyo aadam
Aadam jo dam tu

Chalo to aasmaan vekhun
Maula Ali pasun
Aasmaan midyo taara
Taaran mein chandra tu

Chalo to masjid vekhun
Maula Ali pasun
Masjid midyo mehraab
Mehraab jo harb tu

Chalo to mandir vekhun
Maula Ali pasun
Mandir midyo moorat
Moorat jo soorat tu

Chalo to dariya vekhun
Maula Ali pasun
Dariya midyo laharun
Lahariyan mein laal tu

Chalo to kashti vekhun
Maula Ali pasun
Kashti midyo raahib
Raahib jo saahib tu

~

The Lord Has Come Home / Hivde Sukh Barse

Hove re deeghi deeghi paal samand ri
Talve jal Jamuna ro neer, haan
Hove re paal chadhe guru no main joviyo re
Satguru tramana ri seer, haan

Hove re aaj saahib maun ghar praamana re
Hivde sukh barse anand, haan

Hove re kesar gaar gadhaavna re
Moteeda ro chauk puraaun, haan
Hove re chandan ro chauk guru ro baisno
Doodh paga na guru ra paaun, haan

Hove re aangan ropaaun elchi re
Vadh rahi amar bel, haan
Hove re phoolada ro mukut banaavno re
Hivde re koonpal mel, haan

Hove re teen lok Hari no main khojiyo re
Hari melya neda najeek, haan
Hove re bhagat mugat re kaarane re
Keh gaya Das Kabir, haan

~

My Girlhood Home / Naiharva

Naiharva hamka na bhaavai
Saain ki nagari param ati sundar, jahaan koi jaaye na aavai
Chaand sooraj jahaan pavan na paani, ko sandes pahunchaavai
Darad yah saain ko sunaavai

Aage chalo panth nahin soojhe, peechhe dosh lagaavai
Kehi vidhi sasure jaaun mori sajni, virah jor jaraavai
Vishay ras naach nachaavai

Bin satguru apno nahin koi jo yah raah bataavai
Kahat Kabira suno bhai saadho, sapne nu peetam aavai
Tapan yah jiya ki bujhaavai

~

The House of Love (set of couplets)

Yeh to ghar hai prem ka,
khaala ka ghar naahin
Sees utaare bhoin dhare,
tab baithe ghar maanhi

Kabir ka ghar shikhar pe,
silhali si gel
Paanv na tike papeel ka,
kyun manva laade bail

Dubki maari samoond mein,
ja niksa aakaas
Gagan mandal mein ghar kiya,
vahaan heera paaya daas

Paanch tatva teen gun ke
aage mukti mukaam
Jahaan Kabir saah ghar kiya,
vahaan Gorakh, Dutt na Raam

2. SONGS OF THE PATH

You've Been Walking for Ages / Chaalat Chaalat Jug Bhaya

Ji Kabira re
Chaalat chaalat jug bhaya
Kaun bataave dhaam ji?
Mann bhedun ko vhaala bhoolo phire
Paanv kos par dhaam ji

Ji Kabira re
Kaun matki kaun jherna re
Kaun bilovanhaar ji?
Mann matki tan jherna re
Surat bilovanhaar ji

Ji Kabira re
Ghrit Kabiro sant le gayo re
Chhaachh piye sansaar ji
Ghrit liya to vhaala kya hua re?
Dhen dhani re paas ji
Poola neeru nij prem ra re
Duvo din raat ji

Ji Kabira re
Surat baan bhami rahyo re
Jhel sake to jhel ji
Soora hove to re sanmukh ladiye
Nahin kaayar ro khel ji

Ji Kabira re
Sooli ke upar ghar hamaara
Oth paayo vishraam ji
Kabiro sant rami rahyo re
Aath pahar hoshiyaar ji

~

If You Really Want / Jo Teri Ichha

Jo teri ichha tirvaani hoye to
Turant taiyaari kar leeje re, haan haan re
Tan mann dhan arpo re gura ne
Arey, himmat haar mat leeje
Re bhagti raaji hoi ne keeje re, haan haan re
Jo mann thaaro kahyo nahin maane
Dosh gura ne mat deeje, re bhagti…

Pehla dil apno karmoye to
Peechhe paanv mat deeje re, haan haan re
Satguru shaame mukti ra daata
Unka sharanon mein reeje, re bhagti raaji hoi…

Ingla pingla sukhman joya
Ghar sukhman ko tu leeje re, haan haan re
Ajapa jaap japo sumiran ka,
unmun aasan leeje, re bhagti raaji hoi…

Oham soham ki rachna tu dekhi le
Maain magan hoi ne reeje re, haan haan re
Daduram sadguru sharanon mein
Jeev mugat kar leeje, re bhagti raaji hoi…

~

Climb Slowly, My Friend / Dheera Se Chadhna

Dheere se chadhna mere bhai re hansa
Sambhal ke chadhna mere bhai re hansa
Gir mat jaana mere bhai

Laakh kos aur solah yojan chadhne ki gam naahin
Paanv na tike papeel ka re
Kaise chadhoga mere bhai, re hansa?

Aath paanch nau gotar bahutar undi undi khaai
Is khaai mein gir mat jaana
Bhavsaagar kera maai, re hansa

Aas paas tere surat suhaagan raag chhattees gaayi
Is raagan mein bhool mat jaana
Aava gaman ke maai, re hansa

Raah saankda panth kathin hai chadhna mushkil bhai
Pavan khench ulta chadha le
Beech sushamna ke maai, re hansa

Ramanand mohe satguru mil gaya deenha bhed bataai
Kahein Kabir suno bhai saadho
Aava gaman mit jaai, re hansa

~

The Cart of Meditation Is Tottering / Bhajan Ro Gudak Rahyo Gaado

Bhajan ro gudak rahyo gaado
Kar maalik ne yaad mana
Kun baithyo aado?

Paanch vanaan ri lakdi mangaayi
Das vanaan ri keel
Nav das maas gadhanta laagi
Chaale laakhun meel

Oont bado agyaan
Sat ri saankal ghaale
Nem dharm ra peti patiya
Satguru sabdaan chaale

Le bhaato gharvaali chaali
Prem poorablo thaal
Har bhajiyo gatkaavan laagyo
Hun aayo tu chaal

Raam naam ra geda laagya
Nit nem ra not
Fakru keve kat jaasi
Thaaro janam janam ra khot

~

Drive This Cart Slowly / Zara Halke Gaadi Haanko

Zara halke gaadi haanko,
Mere Raam gaadi waale
Zara dheere dheere gaadi haanko,
Mere Raam gaadi waale

Gaadi meri rang rangeeli
Paiyya hai laal gulaal
Haankan vaali chhail chhabeeli
Baithan vaala Raam, O bhaiyya

Gaadi atki ret mein
Aur majal padi hai door
Ee dharmi dharmi paar utar gaya
Ne paapi chakanachoor, O bhaiyya

Des des ka vaid bulaaya
Laya jadi aur booti
Va jadi booti tere kaam na aayi
Jad Raam ke ghar se chhooti, re bhaiyya

Chaar jana mil mato uthaayo
Baandhi kaath ki ghodi
Leja ke marghat pe rakhiya
Phoonk deenhi jaise holi, re bhaiyya

Bilakh bilakh kar tiriya rove
Bichhad gayi re meri jodi
Kahe Kabir suno bhai saadho
Jin jodi tin todi, re bhaiyya

~

It's All a Game of Come-and-Go / Chala Chali Ka Khela

Sab chala chali ka khela
Do din ka hai jag maan mela
Sab chala chali ka khela

Koi chala gaya, koi jaave
Koi gathdi baandh sidhaave
Koi khada taiyaar akela

Ghar maat pita sab bhai
Tere ant sahaayak naai
Kyon bhare paap ka thaila?

Kar paap kapat chhal maaya
Dhan laakh karod kamaaya
Sang chale nahin ek dhela

Yeh nashvar sab sansaara
Kar bhajan prabhu ka pyaara
Brahmanand kahe sun chela

~

O My Heart, Let's Go Home / Mano Chalo Nija Niketane

Mano, chalo nija niketane
Shangshar bideshe, bidesheri beshe
Bhromo keno okarone?

Bishoyo panchoko aar bhootogono
Shobe tor par, keho noy apano
Poro preme keno hoye ochetono
Bhulicho apono jone

Sottyo pothe mon koro arohono
Premer alo jali, chalo onukhono
Shangete shombol rekho punnyo dhono
Gopone oti jatane

Shadhu songe naame aachhe pathodham
Shranto hole totha korio bishram
Patho vranto hole, shudhaio potho
Shei patho nibashi jane

Lobho moho adi, pathe doshugono
Pathikero kore shorbosho moshono
Paromo jotone rekhore prohori
Shamo damo duio jone

Jodi dekho pathe, mon, bhoyeri aakar
Praanpone diyo dohaai Raajaar
Shey pathe Raajaar boroi prataap
Shomon domon jaar shaushone

~

No Time for Loitering (set of couplets)

Vethe var na pavan,
sute milan na supireen
Je mathe randan rulan,
saajan mile tinkhe

Je tu kaal mui
Ta kal hi gadhi piriyan khe
Kadahen ka na sui
Ta saghi gadhi sajane

Sad ma kar sadan reey
Halan reey ma hal
Jalan reey ma jal
Rooan reey mataan rui

Jaan jiyen taan jal
Kaanhe jaaye jalan reey
Tateey thaddeey hal
Kaanhe vel vihanji

~

Sweetheart, Dear Girl / Pyaari Sajni Re

Pyaari sajni re, apne piya ne manaai lena
Piyaji to soota sukh bhar neend
Piya ne jagaai lena

Naabhi kamal ke maan, ek naagan jhulo haan
Paanch chor vere laare, jeevlo bujhoyo

Hirday kamal ke maan, ek surta jaagi haan
Chaar purush kiya paas, jeevlo jagoyo

Bhanvar gufa ke maan, ek bhanvaro gunakyo haan
Mahak mahak leve vaas, nindhada kis vidh aave hari?

Magan bhaya hai do nain, tam to piya pal kholo re
Bhadake sun ud gayi mhaari neend, piya hans bolo sahi

Boliya Kabir vichaar, vo to koi nar jaage haan
Aaya aaya guruji re dwaare, bharamna so bhaagi re

~

The Traveller's Come to Take Me Away / Batavado Aayo Leva Ne

Batavado re aayo maan levanana
Mhaane ab ke bachaai de re mori maan

Aath kotdi das darwaaza
Apne mandariye maaye
Lukti re chhipti main phirun re
Lukti na chhode bairido naaye

Haath jod ke bolyo re batavado
Suno re boodhiya baat
Mhaane hukam hai Raam ro
Main aaya modam dhalti raat

Haath jod kar boli re boodhiya
Suno praamana baat
Mhaari kanya rah gayi raman ri
Sang ri saheliyaan re saath

Satre din saavan ka gaya
Hame aayi teej parbhaat
Mhaari kanya baali re bholi
Ab ke kar do ne gunaah maaf

Saat saheladi sab kar aaye
Goonthan laage sheesh
Sheesh goonth ne boli boodhiya
Devo mhaari kanya ne seekh

Paanch bhaaya ri benadi re
Dharyo sheesh par haath
Kutumb kabeelo yaan rahyo re
Koi nahin chaalyo re un re saath

Kahat Kabira sun bhai saadhu
Maano hamaari baat
An saasariyo sab ne jaano
Bhaj lo Hari ro naam

3. TOUGHEN UP

Devotion's Tough, My Friend! / Lagan Kathin Hai

Lagan kathin mere bhai guruji se,
lagan kathin mere bhai
Lagan lage bina kaaj na sarihai,
jeev parlay ho jaai

Swati boond liye ratat papeehara,
piya re piya rat laai ho
Pyaase praan jaaye kyon na ab hi,
aur neer nahin bhaayi

Do dal aan jude hain jab sanmukh,
soora let ladaai
Took took hoye gire dharani pe,
khet chhod nahin jaayi

Mirga naad shabd ka bhedi,
shabad sunan ko jaayi
Soyi ho shabad sun praan daan de,
tanik na mann mein daraayi

Chhodo apne tan ki aasa,
nirbhay hoi gun gaayi ho
Kahein Kabir aisi lau laavo,
sahaj milega guru aai

~

Love-Water Does Not Stay / Raakhite Naarili Premojol

Ae kaancha haadite
Raakhite naarili premojol
O khyapa re!

Kaancha haadi jole dile
O mon jaaibe gule
Tokhon laagi jaabe
Bheeshon gondogol

Korbi jodi paaka haadi
Tobe chole jaabi gurur baadi
Shetha premagune shiddho hobi
Roope korbi jholomol jholomol

Goshai Shadanando bhebe aaul
Khyapa Manohar tui hobi ki baul?
Dhaan kootile hobe chaaul
Boli thoosh kootile ki ba phol?

~

Practise It to Have It / Amal Kare So Paai

Amal kare so paai, ho saadhu bhai
Amal kare so paai
Jab lag amal nasha nahin karta
Hey, tab lag maja nahin aai

Aandho haath liye kar deepak,
kar parkaash dikhaai
Auran ke aage kare chaandna,
aap andhera ke maai

Aandho aap andar nahin darse,
jag mein bhalo kehvaai
Doodh pootra daani re ban ke,
paakhand pet bharaai

Kaazi pundit pach pach haara
ved kuraan ke maanhi
Bhaniya re guniya samjhat naahin,
ya ne kun samjhaai?

Guru sharan mein maali likhe Likhmo,
sab santan kera maanhi
Hai koi aisa phakkad jag mein,
apno amal jamaai?

~

If You Want to Reach / Mon Jodi Tui

Paagol mon!
Mon jodi tui Brindaabone jaabi
Anuraager ghore maarga chaabi

Tolatoler moddhe diya
Urdhoreta shaadho giya
Nittoshiddha hobi
Prokriti hole dhorte paare
Pungshajaare naahi paabi

Prokritir shobhaab dhore
Shaadhon koro hobe urdhoroti
Shashanko tui
Koto dine gopi anuga hobi?

~

The Simple, Natural House / Shohojer Ghore

Shohojer ghore shohoj shaadhon je jona kore
Shohoj bhojon jaaye na likhon
Bhojon aachhe ved-bidhi paare

Agni sporsho hoile pore, ghrito jodi naahi gole
Tobe roop roti rosh oojaan chole, botreesh kothaar upore
Shei botreesh kothaar taalaay aata, chaabi bhino na jaaye khola
Roop roshete chaabi aanta, shodor khidki dui dhaare

Ei je shodor khidki ei dui dhaare, shetha roop roti rosh boshot kore
Dekhte hobe nehaar kore, shetha roshoraaj biraaj kore
Roshoraaj she rosher shwaroop, maha bhaab mile hoye aarek roop
Shaakaar bindu aar niraakaar roop, odhor dhora je dhore

Sri Krishno bilaasher shindhu, kollolero ek bindu
Raadharaani aamaar poorno bindu, gopigone bindu bindu
Paan kore joto bhokto bindu, kaam bindu jogot shongshaare

Jaadu Bindu bolchhe sposhto jaar je bhaab shei she shrestho
Aar noshtheek hole pore totha bostu bichaar kore
Joto upaaye toto oddhyaaye, shindhu kobhu naahi shukhaaye
Benga tooni paan kore

~

Persuade Your Heart / Mana Ke Manai Le

Thaara mana ke manai le ji
Eena dil ke samjhaai le ji
Mana ke manai le, ike samjhaai le
Thodo ee ne manai le ji

Daaru mat peejo re veera
Gaanja mat peejo re veera, beedi mat peejo re veera
Ya se bhakti to nahin hove ji
Naam ka katora kaise piyoge, mhaara veer?

Ved puraan ka re veera,
Bhaav bhajan ka re veera, saakhi shabad ka re veera
Tam to gaanthadliya mat baandho ji
Mool haath nahin aayo re, mhaara veer

Kori kori aankh tori, ya mein kaajaliyo mat melo ji
Naina ko roop yo bigaadiyo re, mhaara veer

Haath maay deevlo re veera, daforiya ne nahin soojhhe ji
Rain andhaari mein kaise chalyoga, mhaara veer?

Guru charana mein re veera, Roopa ko raani bolya ji
Bhaati hukum ki cheli, mhaara veer

~

No One Is Yours / Koi Nahin Apna

Koi nahin apna, samajh mana

Dhan daulat tera maal khajeena
Do din ka sapna, samajh mana

Nanga aana, nanga jaana
Nahin kapda rakhna, samajh mana

Trikoodi mein se jaan nikal gayi
Munh per daalo dhakna, samajh mana

Chaar jan mil ke khatiya uthaana
Jangal beech rakhna, samajh mana

Jangal man laayi lakad ki mauli
Koi unse phoonkna, samajh mana

Kahat Kabira suno bhai saadho
Vo hi ghar hai apna, samajh mana

~

Why Wander Outside? / Baahar Kyon Bhatke?

Thaaro Raam hirday maanhi,
baahar kyon bhatke?

Aisa aisa heerla ghat maan kahiye
Jauhari bina heero kon paarkhe?

Aisa aisa ghrit doodh maan kahiye
Bina jhugiye maakhan kaisa nikle?

Aisa aisa aag lakdi maan kahiye
Bina ghasiye aag kaisa nikle?

Aisa aisa kivaad hivde par jadiya
Gura bina taala kon khole?

Kahat Kabir suno bhai saadho
Raam mile thaane kon hatke?

~

Tear Out These Eyes (set of couplets)

Ubharande sij saan,
pireen je na pasandiyun
Kadhi khe kaaga,
nevaala nain deeyaan

Akhiyun sei dhaar
jain se pase piriyan khe
Bedaan keen manihaar
ghanu risaaro supireen

Akhiyan mein achi ve,
ta vaare aaun dhakiyaan
Tokhe na dise deh,
ne aaun na pasaan ko byo

Jaan jaan pase paan khe,
taan taan na hai sajood
Vinyaaye vajood,
tihaanpo takbeer chyo

~

The King's Head (set of couplets)

Allah ji aas kare chaaran chorein chang
Janaavar jangal ja kan rehaanu rang
Beejal sandho bang khaalik khaali na kareen

Allah ji aas kare hali aayo heen
Maal na mange manganu yaachak mange ji
Vadh velo thi aaun saahat sabar na sahaan

Allah ji aas karein hali aaye hoon
Tu ooncho mathe arsh aaun bhoro mathe bhoon
Kya tusandhe tu aaun svaali sir jo?

Mahalein aayo mangano, khani saaju siri
Lage tandu tamboor ji, piya kot kiri
Handhe maagein hui thi tuhinji, Beejal, daanaham buri
Sisi tanahi sultaan khaan, achi ghot ghuri
Jhoonaag dah jhuri, poondin jahaain jharok mein

4. A SAVAGE MOCKERY

The World Has Gone Mad / Saadho Dekho Jag Bauraana

Saadho, dekho jag bauraana
Saach kaho to maaran dhaave, jhoothe jag patiyaana

Hindu kahat hai Raam hamaara, Musalmaan Rahmaana
Aapas mein dou lade marat hain, marm koi nahin jaana

Bahut mile mohe nemi dharmi, praat karein asnaana
Aasan maar dimbh dhar baithe, mann mein bahut gumaana

Maala pahire topi pahire, chhap-tilak anumaana
Bahutak dekhe peer auliya, padhein kitaab kuraana
Karein mureed kabar batalaavein, unhun khuda na jaana

Ya vidhi hansat chalat hain hamko, aap kahaavein syaana
Kahe Kabira suno bhai saadho, inmein kaun deewaana?

~

It's All Lies / Baad Bade So Jhootha

Baad bade so hi jhootha, pundit bhai
Haan jhootha re, baad bade so hi jhootha
Raam ke kahe se jagat gati paave,
to khaand kahe mukh meetha
Baad bade so hi jhootha, haan pundit bhai

Pavak kahe se paanv jo daaye, jal kahe trishna bujhaai
Bhojan ke kahe se bhookh jo bhaage, to duniya tar jaai

Nar ke sang sua Hari bole, Hari partaap na jaane
Jo kabahu ud jaaye jangal, to Hari surta na aade

Bin dekhe, bin aras paras, bin naam liye kya hoi?
Dhan ke kahe se dhanik jo hove, to nirdhan rahega na koi

Saachi preet vishay maaya se Hari darshan ki aa phaansi
Kahein Kabir ek Raam bhaje bin, baandhe jampur jaasi

~

Your Body's a City / Thaari Kaya Nagar

Thaari kaaya nagar ka kun dhani, maarag mein loote paanch jani
Paanch jani, pachees jani, maarag mein loote paanch jani

Aasha trishna nadiyaan bhaari, beh gaya sant bada brahmachaari, hare hare
Vo ubarya jo sharan tumhaari, chamak rahi hai sel ani

Ban mein lut gaye munijan nanga, das gayi mamta ulta taanga, hare hare
Jaake kaan guru nahin laaage, sringi rishi par aan padi

Saadhu sant mil roke ghaata, saadhu chadh gaya ulti baata, hare hare
Gher liya sab aughat ghaata, paar utaaro aap dhani

Indra bigaadi Gautam naari, Kubja bhayi gaya Krishna muraari, hare hare
Radha Rukhma bilakhti haari, Raam chandra par aan bani

Shankar lut gaye nejadhaari, raiyyat unki kaun bichaari, hare hare
Bhool rahi karman ki maari, teen yug jhuk rahi teen jani

Saaheb Kabir guru deenha hela, Dharamdas suno nij chela, hare hare
Lamba maarag panth duhela, simro sirjanhaar dhani

~

They've Sucked Allah Dry (set of couplets)

Mullon mujhaavar machhlo
Ae tei hikdi jaat
Vejhi haddo vaat
Ini dhutiyo Allah ke

Mullah mullah ma cho
Ihe aahedi aaheen
Miru sandhe maah te pya maanak mataayeen
Ehada ee aaheen
Laalti Latif chae

Mullah Mullah ma cho
Ae khaalik khalkiyaain khar
Ae pinan te ta pet bhareen
Je deh manjh dachar
Inhi khareliyan ta khar
Keeh na lahendo Latif chae

Mullah mullah ma cho
Ae akhiyun hondehi andha
Laaye chhad Latif chae
Nee khaneeyin ja khanda
Seda ae sandha ini na sunyaato saiyyad chae

~

You Lost Your Caste, They Shout / Jaat Gailo Bole

Jaat gailo jaat gailo bole
Ae ki ajob karkhana?
Shatya kaaje keu noi raaji
Shobhi dekhi ta na na na

Aashbaar kaale ki jaat chhile?
Eshe tumi ki jaat nile?
Ki jaat hoba jaabaar kaale?
Ae kotha bhebe bolo na

Brahmon chondal chamar muchi
Ek jole shab hoi go shuchi
Dekhe shune hoi na ruchi
Jome to kaakeo chhaadbe na

Gopone je beshyaar bhaat khaaye
Tate dhormer ki khoti hoye
Lalon bole jaat kare kohe
Ee bhorom to gailo na

~

Go Ask Your Guru / Koi Poochho Apne Guru Se

Koi poochhat apna guru se
Yo bolo yo nar kaun purush hai, hare hare
Koi kahe yo jeev bole, hare hare
Koi kahe kartaara
Yo kartaar base ghat bheetar
To kaahe mare sansaara?

Yo jeev to sab mein bole, hare hare
Jhaad bindu ban raaya
Paanch tatva se nyaara khele
Rang nahin vaake roopa

Yaan gadh parvat se patthar mangaaya, hare hare
Dai taanchi ghadhavaaya
Eena dev mein kala jo hoti
To ghadhva vaala ne khaata

Ghadhyo dev ghadha mein bole, hare hare
Anghadh ka ausaara
Ek din baabo anghadh jaage
To ghadhya dev ne bhaage

Kahe Kabir suno bhai saadho, hare hare
Yo path hai nirbaana
Eena panth ki kare khojna
Aava gaman mit jaana

~

Where's Paradise, My Friend? / Vaikunth Kahaan Hai?

Vaikunth kahaan mere bhai, jahaan base niranjan raai
Vaikunth kahaan mere bhai

Ajgar tattoo bajgar dole, kaun mahal mein jaai
Kitna ooncha kitna neecha, kitni hai gehraai?

Baithi gauva kabhi na uthaai le ganga nahvaai
Khol dupatto aansu poonchhe, chaara charo meri maai

Aadha sarag tak pahuncha hansa, phir maaya gher laai
Lekar boodhali narak kund mein, phir chauraasi paai

Chun chun gagri odhe dupatta, chaal nirkhe vo saain
Chaar padaarath visaar deenha, mukti tanik na aai

Koi Hindu koi Turk kahaave, koi baaman baniyaai
Uda suva jab chala pinjara, ek varan ho jaai

Aundha aaya aundha jaaya, aundha liya bulaaai
Kahe Kabir aundhi ka jaaya, kabahi na seedha hoi

~

Leave Your Charades, O Yogi / Latko Chhod De

Latko chhod de jogiya
Badale ri daali heendo maandiyo, jogi rajaji
Tale lagaai aag, latko chhod de
O jogi rajaji, asal fakiri dhaar

Nhaaya-dhoya Hari na mile, har koi leve nhaaye
Jal mein nhaave maachhli, kad amraapur jaaye?

Moond mundaaya Hari na mile, har koi leve mundaaye
Chhathe maheene mundeeje bhedadi, kad amraapur jaaye?

Jata badhaaya Hari na mile, har koi leve badhaaye
Jata badhaave van mein reechhda, kad amraapur jaaye?

Nath Gulabi milya guru poora, poore mann ki aas
Abke hele taar do, jas gaave Bhavani Nath

~

O Mullah, What Would You Know? (set of couplets)

Ve mullah, tu ki Muhammad di shaan jaane?
Shaan puchhni ha taan, Hussain tun puchh
Ya puchh Hazrat Uwais kanu
Ya Bilal kanu ya Ali Karbala tun puchh
Tu baaz aaja ina harkataan tun
Be-adbiyaan karan ton chukda nahin
Teriyaan lambiyaan namazaan nu ki kariye
Je tu dar Muhammad de jhukda nahin?

Namaz padhe te kam janaana, te roza sarfa roti
Uchchiyaan vaangaan denden jede niyat rakhenden khoti
Haj padhan ku o venden, onde ghar de kam tun khoti
Peer Bulleshah je rab nu milna, tu khol andar di kothi

Padh padh aalam faazil baneyo
Kadi apne aap nu padheyaai nahin
Bhaj bhaj vadadaae mandir maseeti
Kadi dil apne tu vadeyaai nahin
Ivein roz shaitaan naal ladadaae
Kadi nafz apne naal ladeyaai nahin
Asmaani udadiyaan fadadaae, Bulleya
Jeda ghar baitha onu fadedayaai nahin

~

You Didn't Sing Govind's Name / Govindo Gaayo Nahin

Govindo gaayo nahin,
tune kya kamaayo baanware?

Ahran ki chori kari re, kiyo sui ko daan re
Chadh chaubaare jhaank riyo tu, abhi na aayo maan re

Hindu hokar peepal kaate, kharch kanya ko khaaye re
Muslim hokar byaaj kamaave, jada mool se jaaye re

Ganga tu nhaayo Gomti re, chadhyo gadh Girnar re
Banjaare re bail taain thaaro, gayo jamaaro haar re

Baith patthar ki naav banaai, chhodi jal ke beech re
Kahat Kabir suno bhai saadho, doobela majhdhaar re

~

These Guys Know Nothing / Ee Nahin Jaane

Ee ni jaane, kachhu ni jaane, ni jaane guru maala re mein
Jab lag peri, jab lag pheri, todiya phenk di jaala mein

Eena kutra ne kaanch bataayo, oobhi aayo un chaala mein
Baahar bheetar deesan laage, bhookhi rayo galiyaara mein

Eena baandara ke heero re mal gyo, ni jaane una moti re mein
Khaaro meetho laago chaakhvo, dhari layo mukh aalya mein

Eeni bhains padmini ke gaino pairaayo, va ni jaane gaino re mein
Dai re ramalko bhaagi lautva, loti rai nij gaara mein

Uni gadhada ke ganga ji lai gaya, oo ni jaane una teerath mein
Kahe Kabir suno bhai saadho, loti rayo nij ghooda mein

~

Who Cares for You, Formless God? / Angadhiya Deva

Koi nahin karega thaari seva
Angadhiya deva, koi nahin karega thaari seva

Ghadiya ghaat ke sab koi dhaave
Nit uthlaave seva
Pooran brahm akhandit swaami
Jinko jaane na koi bheva

Brahma Vishnu Maheshwar kahiye
In sir laagi kaai
Inke bharose koi mat rehna
Inhone mukti na paai

Das avataar niranjan kahiye
Vo apna nahin hoi
Vo to apni karni bhoge
Karta aur hi koi

Jogi jati aur sati sanyaasi
Aap aap mein ladiya
Kaheiṅ Kabir suno bhai saadho
Shabd lakhe so tariya

~

The Fish Is Thirsty in Water / Paani Mein Meen Pyaasi

Ho santon bhai
Paani maan meen pyaasi
Sun sun aave maula haansi
Paani maan meen pyaasi

Aatam gyaan bina nar bhatke
Kau Mathura kau Kaasi?
Mrig ke naabhi basat kastoori
Ban maan phirat udaasi

Jaako dhyaan dhare vidhi harihar
Munijan sahas athaasi
Jo tere ghat maan hi viraaje
Param purush avinaasi

Jal beech kamal, kamal beech kaliyaan
Ta par bhanvar nivaasi
Jo mann bas trilok bhayo hai
Japi ho tapi sanyaasi

Hai haajir ko door bataave
Door ki baat niraasi
Kahat Kabira suno bhai saadhu
Guru bina bharam na jaasi

5. THE WORLD AS MARKETPLACE

Row Along the Banks of This River / Nodeer Kinaar

Nodeer kinaar diye beye jaao, monua byapaari
Tomaare moner kotha aami jaai jaanaiya
Haan re haan, monua byapaari

Jonmo loiya ae jogote
Aamaar naai kono baashona
Baashona tel diya shokaal shaanjhe
Diyechi prodeep jaalaiya re

Jemon shikha uthe upor paane
Aamaar ohom sholta puraiya
Ek ek prodeepe shokol jogot
Dilo aala jaalaiya re

Honsha chole shei nodite
Jetha tumi jaao naau baiya
Oshe neer chhadiya khaaye re kheer
Porome porom jaania re

~

The Cup Is Full / Bharyo Raam Ras Kaanso

Yahaan bharyo Raam ras kaanso, re bhanwara
Tu mat jaaje re pyaaso, haan re

Yo Raam ras mole na beeke,
bah rahyo baaraho maaso, haan re
Sugura hoye so bhar bhar peeve,
nugura jaave re pyaaso

Laagi bajariya tu sauda re kar le,
paav rati chaahe maaso
Saudaagir ne sauda re kar liya,
moorakh phire udaaso

Is takdi mein pher nahin koi,
sant hoi ne dekho
Tan ki taaraju mein toli ke dekho,
paav ghate na maaso

Raam ratan dhan saame re bharya,
chatur hoi ne chaakho
Kahe Kabir suno nar bhedi,
moorakh jaave pyaaso

~

Drink the Wine of Hari's Name / Hansa Piyo Re Piyaala

Hansa chaalo satguruji na des maan ji
Jiyaan kaag palti ne hans hoye re
Hansa bijliyaari jhalmal hui rahya ji
Tiyaan mehuliya varse re akhand dhaar re

Hansa piyo re piyaala Hari re naam ra ji
Ae maan aava gaman mati jaaye re
Hansa piyo re piyaala nirbhay naam ra ji

Hansa agar chandan kera hal vale ji
Te maan vaavyo motida no beej re
Hansa motida ugyo Hari je naam ro ji
Jene sheel santon seenchan haar re

Hansa motida padyo maidan maan ji
Jene jagat ulaanghi ne jaaye re
Hansa jyaare aave re heerla na paarkhu ji
Taiyaan heerla vechaaye monge mol re

Hansa kaaya re nagar kere sheher maan ji
Ae maan ulti ne sulti baajaar re
Hansa aap saudaagar hui rahya ji
Taiyaan vaanajo heera moti laal re

Hansa aavant jaavant Hari ne odkho ji
Te maan vaar na pher lagaar re
Hansa Dev Dungarpuri boliya ji
Je ja dhan ghadi ne dhan bhaag re

~

If You Wish to Receive / Lena Hue So

Lena hue so leeje mhaara bhaida re
Ab aayi to levan ki re bela re saadho
Maanakho janam heero haath nahin aave re
Phir bhatkat chauraasi ra phera re saadho
Edo ratan heero haath nahin aave re

Shyaam jata sir shvet bhayi hai re
Tane ajeyun na aave laaja re saadho
Tirya jake nar karni su tir gaya re
Ab sariya jaka ra kaaja re saadho

Gyaan kathe nar rehni nahin rehta re
Bin to rehni kaisa gyaana re saadho?
Mann parmod sake nahin apno re
Vo to auraan su poochhe myaana re saadho

Hansa hue so hans gati haale re
Ab chheelar paanv na mele re saadho
Saadh hue mhaare ghat ujiyaala re
Ve to akel kala maanhi khele re saadho

Sheesh utaar dharyo gura aage re
Ab kuchh sanshay naahin re saadho
Paancha ne pakdi ek kar leena re
Anubhav aatam maanhi re saadho

Kirpa bhayi jad sauda rachiya re
Ab bhaav bhagat kaisi aasi re saadho?
Rohal ratan amolak paayo re
Ab sir saate avinaashi re saadho

~

My Darling Awareness / Meri Syaani Surta

Mhaari syaani surta
Raam ras pyaalo jhel ri
Raam naam tu bol ri
Antar ka parda khol ri
Mhaari laadli surta

Kar le naabhi kamal se het ri
Mhaara satguru maandi haatadi
Bhaav bhakti ka sauda kar le
Sab rang lag jaave haath ri

Kar le gagan mandal ki sel ri
Mhaara saahib ka rang mahal mein re haan
Ratan gadh mein ratan nipje
Heero lag jaave haath ri, re haan

Chadh ja gagan mandal ka gel ri
Mhaara saahib ra partaap se re
Jhilmil jhilmil jyot barse
Chadhe agam ka gel re

Kar le Raam naam se het ri
Bhakturam aades hai re haan
Satrah khand ke paar khand hain
Un jogiya ko des ri

~

Why? / Kaahe Re?

Kaahe re?
Ghini mili achhahu keesa
Kaahe re?

Aapna maamse harina bairi
Khana naha chhaadaha Bhusuku aheri

Teena na chhupai harina peebai na paani
Harina harineer nilaya na jaane

Harini bolau sun harina tu
Ae ban chhaadi ho hu bhaanto
Tarangate harinaar khur na dissaavai
Bhusuku bhanai moodhahi ahi na paisai

~

My Business Is with God / Mujhe Hai Kaam Ishwar Se

Kutumb parivaar sut dwaara
maal dhan lokan ki
Hari ke bhajan karne se,
agar toote to tootan de

Mujhe hai kaam ishwar se,
jagat roothe to roothan de

Baith sangat santan ki,
karun kalyaan main apna
Lok duniya bhogon mein,
mauj loote to lootan de

Prabhu ke dhyaan dharne-se,
lagi lagan mere dil mein
Preet sansaar vishayon mein,
agar toote to tootan de

Dhari sir paap ki matki,
mere gurudev ne jhatki
Vo Brahmanand ne patki,
agar phoote to phootan de

6. THE TRUTH OF SUFFERING

Look What I've Done / Eda Main Kaam Kiya

Kori kori matki maan thando jal paani
Vohi paani dhol diya
Ramanand, eda main kaam kiya

Oghan bodh kiya
Ramanand, khota main kaam kiya

Bhariyo re samdariye maan gauva roki
Bachhada main rol diya

Itro re jug main to nirkhyo nevna se
Pag pag paap kiya

Brahman ji ra main khadiya re khosya
Teepna main phaad diya

Kahat Kabira re sun bhai saadho
Charana maan sheesh diya

~

Youth and Wealth / Joban Dhan

Joban dhan praamana re doi din chaara
Jero garav mat karo re ganvaara

Haad re maans ra banya re pinjara
Bheetar bharya re bhangaara
Upar rang suchang chadhaaya
Kaarigar hai kiltaara

Pashu re chaam ra banya re panaiya
Naubat banya re nagaara
Nar teri chaam kaam nahin aave
Bad jal hua re angaara

Das sheesh jero bees bhujaava
Riddhi siddhi bahu parivaara
Eva re nar garab maan gal gaya
Lanka ra pati sirdaara

Ae re sansaar, vhaala, sapne ri maaya
Sukrat karo re vyavahaara
Kahat Kabir suno bhai saadho
Bhav jal se utro paara

~

The Disease Called Worry / Chinta Roger

Chinta roger
Aushadh kichhu aasheni shongshaare
Tora bole de aamaare

Probhaate nisheethe chinta
Chinta diprohore
Chinta re chhaad le aamaaye
Chintaaye to na chhaade

Chinta hoite chita bhaalo
Chitaai mora maanoosh poore
Jeeyonte jaalaiya maare
Chintaaye jaare chha thaare go

Shorot bole chinta chhaada
Keho naai shongshaare
Jaari chinti le jaaye bhobo chinta
Tumi chinta koro taare go

~

How Frail Your Body / Kaachi Chhe Kaaya Thaari

Kaachi chhe kaaya thaari, jhuthdi chhe maaya Raam
Jhuthda sa lekh likhaaya Raam Raam Raam
Kaachi ho, kaun ghadeli thaari kaya ho ji ji ji

Ghat hi mein Ganga Raam
Ghat hi mein Jamuna Raam
Ghat hi mein teerath nhaaya Raam Raam Raam

Ghat hi mein taala Raam
Ghat hi mein kunji Raam
Ghat hi mein kholan-haara Raam Raam Raam

Ghat hi mein amba Raam
Ghat hi mein ambli Raam
Ghat hi mein sevanhaara Raam Raam Raam

Machhinder prataap jati
Gorakh bole
Samjhya so hi nar paaya Raam Raam Raam

~

Friends, Be on Your Way / Shartiyun Aain Taan

Shartiyun aain taan vinyodi vinyo la
Muinjhodi pech Punhal saan
Muinjhodi lekh lakhan taan

Allah miyaan,
Uth Aari Jaam ja la
Daaghan daan diyodi diyo la

Allah miyaan,
Hede sheher Bhambhor mein la
Med miskeen ji manyodi manyo la

Allah miyaan,
Adhiyun Shah Latif chain la
Andhar aavaan laaye unyodi unyo la

~

The Mountain Burst into Flames (set of couplets)

Sasui khe sooran ja van van heth valaad
Kare pand pahaad pairan ladhain Punhal jo

Dukh lago doongar bariyo,
bhenar khaani bhun
Mana laatho mu,
sando jiyan aasiro

Shartiyun aghiyun sujhe sunya,
mataan ko mun saan haale
Hik paani na he byo pand ghanu,
hek raaho aahe sunya
Mataan maro unya,
diyo paaraato munjhe Punhal khe

7. LONGING

I Haven't Met My Love (set of couplets)

Aaun na gadhi piriyan khe hi pan deenh vyo
Nihode naabhan sain mukhe neenh niyo
Muthiy maut thiyo peeu peeu kandhe pandh mein

Aaun na gadhi piriyan khe sau sein sij vya
Halan ver hiyaan dekhe chhaal dham diyaan

Aaun na gadhi piriyan khe tu thau lahein sij
Heje diyaan saneho, nehi piriyan khe dij
Vanyi kech chaij, ta vechaari vaat mui

Aaun na gadhi piriyan khe mudiyo sij mathaan
Doh mun dukheey jo hot vinyaayem hathaan
Hoo neen natha piriyein mulk paheenje

Aaun na gadhi piriyan khe vichaeen sij vyo
Baarindiyas baaroch laye doongar manjh diyo
Jatan dhaariya jyo mun na ghurje jediyun

~

To Attain Your Holy Feet / Sri Charon Paabo

Sri charon paabo bole re
Bhobokule daake deen heen kangaale

Srishti kore aatto roshe
Kaar ba doshe bhober kule pathaaile
Ore kaar bhaabe bhobe eshe
Behaal beshe doyaal naam deen bhulaayile

Baanchha kalpotoru naamti dhoro
Baam naai karo shoone elaam shaadhur kule
Tomaar doyaal naamer ki mohima
Jaabe jaana aamaare na toraaile?

Goshaai Heeruchander charon hoye na shoron
Bhojonheen Panju bole ehe
Shei doyaal naamer ae mohima
Jaabe jaana aamake na choron dile

~

O Dark One, Come Quickly / Saanvara Bega Aajo

Bega aajo re Raam ji, beg padhaaro re
Harihar bega aajo
Mhaari maala ra maniyaar, Raam ji bega aajo re
Mhaari kaaya ra kartaar, Harihar jhatpat aajo re

Kaan lagaai der saanvara bega aajo re
Raam ji beg padhaaro ji
Mhaari maala ra maniyaar, saanvara bega aajo re

Thaara kaaran re Raam ji handa bharaaya re
Baap ji nhaavan aajo, saanvara bega aajo
Joun thaari baat baap ji, beg padhaaro re

Thaara kaaran re saanvara bhojan banaayo re
Baap ji jeeman aajo, saanvara bega aajo
Joun janam ki baat haajri likh leejo re

Thaara kaaran re saanvara jhaari bharaai re
Baap ji peevan aajo, saanvara peevan aajo
Mhaari maala ra maniyaar, Raam ji bega aajo re
Joun janam ki baat haajari likh leejo re ji

Doi kar jod jati Gorakh bole laaj raakhjo re
Saanvara bega aajo, baap ji beg padhaaro
Joun thaari baat saanvara bega aajo re

~

The Yogis Cast a Spell on Me / Jogeede Na Jaadu Keenha Re

Rain divas mane nindra nahin aave
Ghaayal mrig jyon jeev dukh paave
Mere sabad kataari maari re
Mero panjaro ghaayal keeno re

Jogeede na jaadu keena re
Mero tan man baanche leena re

Ann paani mane kachhu nahin bhaave
Pal pal kshan kshan yaad sataave
Duniya laage khaari re
Maine pyaalo prem ro paayo re

Virah agni mere tan bich laagi
Bhedbhaav ri bharamna bhaagi
Chadh gayi mere prem khumaari
Hriday prem se bheego re

Mor mugat gale bich maala
Mhaane milya Nandji ra laala
Baai Sua no taari re
Mero janam safal kar deeno re

~

My Heart Aches / Tadpe Bin Baalam

Tadpe bin baalam
Mora jiya

Din naahin chain, rain naahin nindiya
Tadap tadap ke bhor kiya

Tan mann more rahat naahin, dolein
Sooni sej par janam jiya

Kahat Kabir suno bhai saadho
Hari peer dukh door kiya

~

Krishna, Do You Ever Think of Me? / Kanhaiya, Yaad Hai Kuchh Bhi?

Ae Kanhaiya, yaad hai kuchh bhi hamaari?
Kahun kya, tere bhoolne ke main vaari!

Mujhe yaad hai vo zara zara
Tumhein yaad ho ke na yaad ho
Yaad hai kuchh bhi hamaari?

Binti main kar kar bamna se poochhi
Pal pal ki khabar tihaari
Paiyaan padi Mahadev ke ja kar
Ari tona bhi kar ke main haari!

Khaak paro logon is byaahne par
Achchhi main rehti kanvaari
Maika mein main 'Hilm' rehti thi sukh se
Arey phirti thi kyon maari maari

~

Can't Be Alone at Home Anymore / Eka Ghore Roite Naari

Aailo borosha re sokhi
Asaado sraabone
Eka ghore roite naari
Bodhua bihone
Bolo baanchibo kemone

Jhoro jhoro jhore baari re sokhi
Maana naahi maane
Syam beena jhore baari
Aamaaro noyone

Moyura moyuri naache re sokhi
Aanondito mone
Din gaile din phire nai aar
Salavate bhoje

~

I'm Not at Peace for a Moment / Saannu Ik Pal Chain Na Aave

Saannu ik pal chain na aave
Sajna tere bina
Saadda kalleya dil naiyo lagna
Sajna tere bina

Kise da yaar na pardes jaave
Vichhoda na kisi de pesh aave

Aa ve kaavaan tainu vaasta rab da
Kadi saadde vi baith banere
La paigaam koi sajna vaala
Ni main shagan manaavaan tere

Rog vijog te shok hajaaraan
Sajna tere naam de
Ho na bhaanve roz qayaamat
Vichhde yaar jinaan de

Raataan nu jagaavaan diya
Hanjva de tel da
Haiyo rabba sajna nu
Chheti kyon nahin melda?

~

Because of You / Aami Tomaaro Laagiya Re

Aami tomaaro laagiya re
Ghar baari chhaadilaam re
Aar shaagar seenchilaam re
Maanek paivaar aashe

O bondhu re!
Tomaar paagol aami re bondhu
Jaane desher lok re
Aar paashan hui maar le chhuri
Abhagineer buke

O bondhu re!
Dukher kopaal shukh hoi lo na
Phiri deshe deshe
Jugol raashe jonma bodhi
Chokher jole bhaashe

O bondhu re!
Nodeer kaachhe koile re dukho
Paani jai ujaiya re
Vriksher kaachhe koile re dukho
Taar paatra jaaye jhuriya

8. THE COMPANY WE KEEP

Not for Half-baked Ones / Aavela Santon Na Laiye

Mhaari heliye, aavela santon na laiye vaarna
Adhuriya ne na de dil na bhed
Mhaari heliye, koi poora mile to parda kholna

Mhaari heliye, jhoothi sangat maan heli na besna
Jema thaara ghatela chhe maan
Mhaari heliye, saachi sangat maan heli besna
Jema thaara vadhela chhe maan

Mhaari heliye, maanas maanas maan ghana antara
Ek chhe shank ne beejo soot
Mhaari heliye, kuaan kuaan maan ghana antara
Ek khaara ne beeja neer

Mhaari heliye, thaara samdar maan meethi veeradi
Is veeradi na nirmal nirmal neer
Mhaari heliye, bhanat Kabira Dharmidas kun
Guruji thi raakho jaaja het

~

Whom Should I Love? / Kin Sang Karaan Sneh?

Heliye
Kin sang karaan sneh?
Sangat bhali dharmi saadh ri
Sangat keeje nirmal saadh ri

Heliye
Baans ugo ina baag maan, tharak rahi ban raay
Aap jale auran ne jaale, agni ghani ang maay

Heliye
Chandan ugo ina baag maan, harakh kare ban raay
Chandan paas main jaaun, aap chandan hoi jaay

Heliye
Dav laago ina baag maan, panchhi baitho aaye
Hamre jalo pankh bahiro, tam udi pare ko jaaye

Heliye
Phal khaada re paan birodiya, ramiya daalo daal
Tam jalo main ubrun, jeevno kitrik baar?

Heliye
Dav bujhyo jhaada metiye, doodhe bootha meh
Kahat Kabir Dharmidas se, nit nit navlo neh

~

Keep Swan-Company / Hans Milya Se Hans Hoi

Hans milya se hans hoi re
Jo tu jode baithe bugaara
Thaare hanso kahvega na koi re, hansa
Hans milya se hans hoi re

Ee hansa hai ksheer koop ra
Neer koop vahaan naahin re
Neer koop mamta ko re paani
Ee tajiya se hans hoi re, hansa

Das avataar shat darshan kahiye
Ved bhanega nar koi re
Varan, chhatteesa, shastra, geeta
Ee tajiya se hans hoi re, hansa

Paanch naam bhavsaagar ka kahiye
Ya se mukti na hoi re
Yo kul chhodo milo satguru se
Sahaje ho mukti hoi re, hansa

Madva hoi ne baitho re mandir mein
Chadhva ki gam naahin re
Dekhan ka saadhu ghana mathdhaari
Va ko Brahm thikaane naahin re, hansa

Teen lok par baitho yam raaja
Baitho baan sanjoi re
Samajh vichaare chadhyo hans raaja
Kaal diyo hai ab roi re, hansa

Ee hansa hai amar lok ra
Aava gavan mein naahin re
Kahein Kabir suno bhai saadho
Satguru sen lakhaai re, hansa

9. KEEP IT TO YOURSELF!

For a Few Days / Kichhu Din

Kichhu din mone mone ghorer kone
Shyamer peerit raakh gopone
Ishaaraaye koibi kotha gothe maathe
Dekhish jeno keu na jaane,
keu na bojhe, keu na shone

Shyamke jokhon porbe mone
Chaaibi kaala megher paane
Rannashaale kaandbi boshe
Bheeje kaath diye unone

Shyamshaayore naaite jaabi
Gaayer boshon bheejbe kene
Shaayore shaator diye aashbi phire
Gaayer boshon bheejbe kene?

Uttor jaabi shaator hobi
Bolbi aami jaai dokhine
Roshik jaane rosher morom
Auroshike jaanbe kene?

~

Don't Make a Big Fuss / Dhoom Karna Mati

Chhauna rehna, dhoom karna re mati
Paapeeda miljo pachaas
Nugaro miljo re mati
Gura peeraan ri dargaah
Miljo jarna ro jati

Chhauna chhauna bistaan gura ji saan laaijo
Pargat karjo re mati
Je kare to marat lok mare
Baapraaijo mati

Heera panna ro banaj halaaijo
Maakhan laaijo re mati
Je lyaave to taaye tapaaye
Ger nahin aave ek ratti

Rohida ro phool kahije ro phootro
Todan jaaijo re mati
Je lyaave tode gun baahiro
Baas nahin aave ek ratti

Aagad nadiyaan behve apaare
Nhaavan jaaijo re mati
Je nhaave to doob marelo
Paar ukle jati sati

Satt maan aavno satt maan jaavno
Satt re baataan re sati
Kahat Kabira sun bhai saadho
Lachhman baado jati

~

No One Understands My Words / Mhaari Boli Lakhe Na Koi

Aaye mhaari heliye
Main to poorabiya poorab des ra
Boli re lakhe nahin re koi
Heliye boli re hamaari so hi lakhe re
Bhaag poorabliya hoye

Amaare mehram ro saadhu koi nahin
Kin saun karaan main sneh?

Aaye mhaari heliye
Kaan to tilada kora bhala hai
Kaan leeje tel kadhaaye
Adhkachri ghaabar
Donon thookon se bhi jaaye

Aaye mhaari heliye
Kadva paana ni kadvi beladi
Phal jera kadva hoye
Sat shabad cheenha
Beli bichhoda hoye

Aaye mhaari heliye
Dav laagyo re beli maan re
Bhayo re beej ro naash
Kahyo re Kabira Dharmidas saun
Pher ugan ri nahin aas

~

The Secret of Song / Bhajan Bhed Hai Nyaara

Re avadhu, bhajan bhed hai nyaara
Koi jaanega jaananhaara, re avadhu

Kya gaave kya likh batlaave,
kya bharmega sansaara
Kya sandhya tarpan ke keenhe,
jo nahin tattva vichaara re avadhu?

Moond mundaaye sir jata badhaaye,
kya tan laaye chhaara
Kya pooja paahan ki keeje,
kya phal kiye aahaara, avadhu?

Bin parichay saahib koi baithe,
vishay ko kare vyavhaara
Gyaan dhyaan ko vo maram na jaane,
baad kare hai ahankaara

Agam athaah maha ati gehra,
beej na khet nivaara
Vahaan so dhyaan re magan hoi baithe,
kaat karam ki achaara

Jinke aahaar sada antar ke,
keval tattva vichaara
Kahein ho Kabir suno ho Gorakh,
taaro sahit parivaara

~

It's Between Me and My Lord / Main Jaanun Mera Allah Jaane

Arre logon tumhaara kya?
Main jaanun mera Allah jaane

Zar maango to bezar hoon
Sar maango to haazir hoon
Mukh modun to kaafir hoon

Chadha Mansoor sooli par
Jo vaakif tha vohi dilbar
Arre mullah janaaza padh

Main hoon dildaar Haidar da
Sachche sardaar Sarvar da
Pilaao jaam kausar da

Vohi ehsaan mujh par kar
Ameer-ul-momin Haidar
Bulleh da saal poora kar

10. ULAT

Words, These Words / Baani Re Baani

Baani re baani mhaara guru ki nishaani
Alakh janmya un din pavan na paani ho, ho ji

Dharti to barse, bheenje aasmaana
Olati ko paani magri samaana ho, ho ji

Chaalega panthi, thaakega baata
Sovega dokariyo ne ghorega rang khaata, ho, ho ji

Dhobi to dhove, salla nichove
Kapda ka upar baagar sookhe ho, ho ji

Kahein ho Kabir, suno re bhai saadhu
Duniya ni jaane mhaari ulti si baani, ho, ho ji

~

By the Side of the Well / Kuen Re Kinaare

Kuen re kinaare avadhu imli si boi re
Jaaro ped machhaliyaan chhaayo hey lo

Ramta jogi ne mhaara
Aades dena re

Kuen re kinaare avadhu hirni si byaayi re
Ho ji paanch miragla laai hey lo

Sasaiyo shikaari avadhu ban khand chaalyo re
Mamta miragli ne maari hey lo

Khoonto to doodhe avadhu, bhains bilove re
Jaaro maakhan birla khaayo hey lo

Sharan Machhandar jati Gorakh bolya re
Jaan khojya vaan paaya hey lo

~

I Saw Fish Climb up a Tree / Jhaad Chadhanta Machhiya

Jhaad chadhanta machhiya re dekhi,
sasle sinh ko daraaya
Keedi kunjal se ladwa re laaga,
kaun jeeta kaun haara?
Thaari kaaya mein!

Paapi apraadhi raaj karanta deetha,
tam dekho dekhanhaara
Thaari kaaya mein!

Samdar keri leher diyaavi,
andhla kahe main dekha
Naaga kahe mera cheer lutaana,
langda kahe main bhaaga

Agni kahe mane taat padat hai,
paani kahe main pyaasa
Anaaj kahe mane khudiya laagi,
ghirat kahe main rookha

Kahat Kabira suno bhai saadho
ee panth birle paaya
Hiye panth ri kare khojna,
seedhe vaikunth aaya

~

Watch This Play, Boy! / Tam Dekho Tamaasha Ladka!

Tam dekho tamaasha ladka
Tam ho re kaaya gadh ka
Tam ho re joona gadh ka

Eeni kaaya mein paancho chela
Haan, haan, saadhu haan!
Vaan soor veer hoye ladta

Bin baadal ek mahulo barse
Haan, haan, saadhu haan!
Vaan beej kadaakad kadke

Bina paanv ek ghoda daude
Haan, haan, saadhu haan!
Vo daude pavan aakaasha

Eeni kaaya mein toto paalyo
Haan, haan, saadhu haan!
Vaan 'tu hi Raam', 'tu hi Raam' karta

Kahein Kabir saah sun bhai saadho
Haan, haan, saadhu haan!
Vaan bhakti daftar chalta

~

The Heart-Secret of This Wandering Heart / Mon Fokiraar Moneri Katha

Mon fokiraar moneri kotha
Aamaar guruji ta jaane re

Shomudrete naai paani baajaare maare dheu
Aamaar baaper jokhon hoye naai jonom
Aamaar byetaar kole bou re

Gaabheer pete hoye naai bolod laangol bikaaye haate
Aamaar chaashaar jokhon hoye naai jonom
Jol khaabaar jechhe maathe re

Madan Shah Fakir bole bhai, laaglo dishe dishe
Aabaar ei kothataar ortho jaanle
Tomaar dishe jaabe chhoote re

~

Time Is Slipping Away / Ber Chalya Mera Bhai

Ber chalya mera bhai, magan hui
ber chalya mera bhai
Raam re naam ro gelo re pakdo,
chhodo ni moorkhaai
chhodo ni ghamandaai

Pehle to guruji ham janmya,
peechhe bada bhai
Dhoom dhaam se pita re janmya,
sabse peechhe maai

Pehle to guruji doodh jamaayo,
peechhe gaay no doi
Bachhada unre rame pet maan,
ghrit bechva gayi

Keedi chaali saasre,
nau mann surmo saath
Haathi unre haath mein,
oont lapeta jaai

Inda re hata bolta,
bachhiya bolya naai
Kahat Kabir sun bhai saadho,
moorakh samjhe naai

~

My Spinning Wheel Chants the Name of Raam / Mhaaro Charkho Bole Raam Naam

Padi boond samandar ke ole,
paani maan ratan nipaaya
Ek achambho aiso saambhdyo,
beti jaayo hai baap

Arji suno hamaari re
Kaaval suno hamaari re
Mhaaro charkho re bole Raam naam
Bhaje tu hi, tu hi, tu hi, tu!

Beti kahe chhe baap ne
Mhaare anjaayo var la
Anjaayo var nahin mile
to thaare mhaare ghar vaas

Charkho re mhaaro ajab rangeelo,
puniyun laal gulaal
Kaantan vaali chhail chhabeeli,
aakaash se taar latkaayi

Pingan pinjaava main gayi thi,
suno pinjaara bhai
Is pinjaare ko kha gayi sajni,
guru gam bataai

Maata bhi mar jaaye, pita bhi mar jaaye,
mar jaaye ghar bhartaara
Ek na mare yeh sajan soothaar,
yo charkha no gadhnaar

Kahat Kabira sun bhai saadhu,
ya charkho kehvaaye
Ya charkha ne jo nar phere,
janam maran mati jaaye

11. GURU

My True Guru Is Calling / Bolaave Satguru Gyaani

Hoon to chaali bharva paani re
Mane bolaave satguru gyaani re

Ae ji mana!
Peehariyo chhodi ne saasariya maan chaali
Mane ghar maan laage have shaani re

Ae ji mana!
Guruji vagar mane ghadeek nahin chaale
Hey mhaari jaati rahi se aa jawaani re

Ae dharti mandal vach maan!
Dharti mandal vache undho vase ami kuaan
Jema bharya se ameeras paani re

Ae ingla ne pingla nu!
Ingla ne pingla nu maarag meli dene maaya
Thaare sushman maaragiya javaanu re

Ae ji mana!
Das Sattar ne aava guru milya gyaani
Mane baatun bataave shaani maani re

~

To Gaze upon My Guru / Guruji Ke Darshan Main Jaasaan

Guruji re darshan main jaasaan
Raam ratan dhan lyaasaan hey lo

Tan mann dhan guruji re arpan
Sheesh ro naarel chadhaasaan hey lo

Hivde naam ro kasoombo jalaasaan
Bhaav ra bhojaniya chadhaasaan hey lo

Adsath teerath guruji re arpan
Parghat Ganga nhaasaan hey lo

Raam naam ri bedi maan baitha
Bhavsaagar tar jaasaan hey lo

Kahat Kabira suno bhai saadho
Amar patto lakh laasaan hey lo

~

No Giver Like the Guru / Guru Sam Daata Koi Nahin

Jag maangan haara,
Guru sam daata koi nahin
Koi nahin ho aisa koi nahin

Kaagaz ki ek naav bani,
jin mein loha apaara
Satguru paar lagaaviya,
koi sant pukaara

Kya raaja kya baadshaah,
sabne haath pasaara
Saat dweep nau khand mein
satguru ka hi pasaara

Apraadhi teerath chaalya,
kya teerath taare?
Kapat daag chhootya nahin,
bahu ang pakhaarya

Kahe Kabir kya kho gaya,
kya dhoondhan haara?
Andhe ko soojhe nahin,
thaara ghat maan hi ujiyaara

~

Guru Shatters the Pitch Darkness / Guru Vinya Ghor Andhaaro

Jal vinya jyot, pavan vinya paani
Al pal vaar lahar laagi mandariya maan

Guru vinya ghor andhaaro mandariya maan
Divle vinya ghor andhaaro mandariya maan

Etleek chhe potli ne padi jaase hethi
Mili jaase maati maaylo gaar re mandariya maan

Seelari nu saanto ne ras bharyo meetho
Guriye guriye ras nyaaro re mandariya maan

Haath maan chhe vaatko ne saaro shahar bhatkyo
Moorakhda ne tel na aale koi udhaaro re mandariya maan

Kahe ho Kabira suno bhai saadho
Naam liyo niraakaaro re mandariya maan
Naam liyo niraadhaaro re mandariya maan

~

The Guru Made the Unknown Known / Satguru Alakh Lakhaaya

Satguru alakh lakhaaya, saadhu bhai
Param prakaash punj gyaan dhan
Ghat bheetar darshaaya, saadhu bhai

Mann buddhi vaani nahin pahunche
Ved kahat sankuchaaya
Aar paar ke ek akhandi
Neti neti keh gaaya

Shiv Sankadik aur Brahma kahe
Hari haath nahin aaya, saadhu bhai
Vyaas Vashisht vichaarat haare
Kou paar nahin paaya, saadhu bhai

Til mein tel, kaashth mein agan
Pay mein ghrit samaaya, re saadhu bhai
Shabad mein arth, padaarath pad mein
Swar mein raag samaaya, re saadhu bhai

Beej mein ankur, taru, jad, shaakha
Paat, phool, phal, chhaaya, re saadhu bhai
Yun aatam mein hai parmaatam
Jeev, bramha aur maaya, saadhu bhai

Jap, tap, nem, vrat aur pooja
Sab janjaal chhudaaya, re saadhu bhai
Kahe Kabir, kripaal kripa kar
Nij swaroop darshaaya, saadhu bhai

~

The Prophet Lies Between the Eyes / Murshid Nainon Beech Nabi Hai

Murshid nainon beech nabi hai

Syaah safed tilon beech taara
Avigat alakh rabi hai

Aaankhi maddhe paankhi chamkai chamkai
Paankhi maddhe dwaara
Tehi dwaar doorbeen laga kai
Utre bhavjal paara

Sunn sahar baas hamaara
Tahun sarvangi jaavai
Saaheb Kabir sada ke sangi
Sabad mahal le aavai

~

The Unbounded Guru (set of couplets)

Satguru mera baaniya,
kar raha banaj bepaar
Bin takdi bin paalne,
tol raha sansaar

Satguru mera soorma,
aur kare shabad ki chot
Maare gola gyaan ka,
to hare bharam ka khot

Satguru chadhe shikaar pe,
haath mein laal kabaan
Moorakh moorakh bach gaye,
koi maara sant sujaan

Koi maare top teer se,
aave dwaadas ghaav
Satguru maare shabad se,
tal mundi ne upar paanv

Kanphoonka guru had ka,
aur behad ka guru aur
Jab behad ka guru mile,
tab lage thikaana thor

Ye sab guru hain had ke,
behad ke guru naahin
Anhad aapo upje,
anubhav ke ghar maanhi

'Haan' kahun to hai nahin,
'Na' bhi kahyo nahin jaaye
'Haan' aur 'na' ke beech mein,
mera satguru raha samaaye

~

I've Found the True Guru / Satguru Mhaane Saacha Mil Gaya

Satguru ji mhaane saacha re mil gaya
Sohang shabad sarbhang bole
Kooda kapat se bair hamaara
Satguru charan maaye chit dole

Makartaar se het laga le
Bank naal paani re peele
Ida pingala donon chhod kar
Beech svaans sumiran kar le

Nau darvaaja khula dekh le
Dasvaan ra jadiya taala
Satguru ji se chaabi re lai le
Dasvaan ri khidki khole

Aar paar ri raah hai shikhar par
Guru shabad ri gam kar le
Karod bhaan ka hua parkaasa
Vahaan diya deepak baati re joi le

Jinko chot lagi shabdon ki
Vi to magan hua phir kya bole?
Kahe Nanak Das suno bhai saadho
Kathin khel birla khele

~

The Guru Gives the Roots / Gyaan Ki Jadiyaan

Gyaan ji jadiyaan dai mhaare sadguru ne
Gyaan ki jadiyaan dai
Va jadiyaan to mhaane laage jo pyaari

Amrit ras se bhari
Ho gura ji ne deenhi gyaan ki jadiyaan dai

Kaaya nagar maanhi ghar ek banglo re
Taan beech gupat dhari

Paanch naag aur pachees naagini
Soonghat turat mari

Eeni Kaali ne bhaaya sab jag khaaya
Sadguru dekh dari

Kahein Kabir saah suno bhai saadho
Le parivaar tiri

~

Your Love Has Made Me Dance / Tere Ishq Nachaaya

Tere ishq nachaaya kar ke thaiyaan thaiyaan
Chheti aavin ve tabeeba, nai taan main mar gaiyaan

Tere ishq ne dera mere dil ich keeta
Bhar ke zeher pyaala main taan aape peeta
Mere kaamil murshid, hun main paar lagaiyaan

Chhup gaya ve sooraj, baahar reh gayi laali
Ve main sadke hovaan, deve murje ve khaali
Peera main bhul gaiyyan, tere naal na gaiyaan

Ais ishq de jhangi vich mor bulenda
Saannu kible te kaabe ton sohna yaar disenda
Saannu ghaayal kar ke pher khabar na laiyaan

Bullehshah nu saddo Shah Inayat de boohe
Jisne sannu puvaaye chole saave te soohe
Jaan main maari hai addi, mil paya hai vahaiya

12. THE NAME

Remember the Name / Lai Re Naam

Lai re naam, lai re naam, naam se tire
Naam bhooli aatma bhamti phire, ji

Baahare ubho mriglo khetar mein chare
Dhani aave dhore ubho, bhajto phire, ji

Aandhade ne maala deeni, phenkto phire
Moorakh haathade heero deeno, dharti dhare, ji

Nugure na neema deeno, kehto phire
Pehere kasturi kapda, tel mein tare, ji

Saadhuda re sang mein jaaye, sudhro phire
Dev Dungarpuri bolya naam se tire, ji

~

Allah Hu Allah

Allah hu Allah
Jalle-shaan Allah

Tu mila bhi hai, juda bhi hai
Tera kya kehna?
Tu sanam bhi hai, khuda bhi hai
Tera kya kehna?
Allah Hu Allah
Jalle-shaan Allah
Tero naam leehe
Meri hove tasalla

Allah tero naam
Tu kisi shakl mein ho
Main tera shaidaai hoon
Tu agar shamma hai, ai dost
Main parvaana tera

Allah hu Allah
Jalle-shaan Allah
Tero naam leehe
Meri hove tasalla

Tu bas tu
Tu Rahim tu Karim
Tu Sattaar tu Gaffaar
Harsu tehaaro hai yeh tajalla
Allah!

~

The Eternal Name / Guruji Ne Diyo Amar Naam

Guruji ne diyo amar naam
Guru to sareeka koi nahin
Alakh bharya hai bhandaar
Kami re jahaan hai nahin

Daata bad-had ugiyo bhaan
Chand taara chhupi gaya
Aisa jap tap jog anek
Naam tale dabi gaya

Aisi laagi samand beech laaye
Jalaaya se na jale
Aisa vaanchoga ved puraan
Naam guru bina na mile

Daata naam sareekoyo daan
Mati deejo re ajaan ne
Ghughu dekhe taara handhi jyot
Vo nahin jaane bhaan ne

Daata chit man chint achet
Rateelo nij naam ko
Aisa sahi sahi keve hai Kabir
Ponchoga nij dhaam ko

~

Meditate, My Friend / Bhajo Re Bhaiya

Bhajo re bhaiya
Raam Govind Hari

Jap tap saadhan
Kachhu nahin laagat
Kharchat nahin ghatri

Santat sampat
Sukh ke kaaran
Ja so bhool padi

Raam naam ko
Sumiran kar le
Sir pe maut khadi

Kahat Kabira
Raam na ja mukh
Ta mukh dhool padi

~

Raam Chants in My Every Vein (set of couplets)

Sab van to tulsi bhaye,
aur parvat shaaligram
Sab nadiyaan Ganga bhayin,
jab jaana aatam Raam

Rag rag mein bole Raam ji,
aur rom rom rarankaar
Sahaje hi dhun upje,
so hi sumiran saar

Maala japun na kar japun,
mukh se kahun na Raam
Raam hamaara hamein jape,
ham paayo bisraam

Raam naam ki loot hai,
loot sake to loot
Ant samay pachhtaayega,
jab praan jaayega chhoot

~

While You Are Well / Jab Lag Sukhiyo Shareer

Hove re bhaag bhala re saadhu
Satguru maliya, padiyo samand maan seer
Hansa re hove chug leejiye re
Naam amolak heer

Hari ra gun gaay le re haan
Saadhu bhai, jab lag sukhiyo shareer
Peechhe re yaad nahin aavse piya
Pinjre mein vyaape peed

Hove re joban hata bhaj leejiye re
Jej nahin karna beer
Vikal budhaapo tane aavse, piya
Manado nahin jhaale dheer

Hove re pal pal kshan kshan aayu ghatat hai
Jyon anjali ko neer
Phir re hanso nahin aavse, piya
Mansarovariye ri seer

Hove re sab devan ro dev Raamaiyo
Sab peeraan ro peer
Kahat Kabira bhaj leejiye re
Sukhsaagariye ri seer

13. OCEAN

I'm at Play / Ochintu Koi Mane

Ochintu koi mane raste male ne kadi
dheere thi poochhe ke kem chhe
To aapne to kahiye ke dariya si mauj maan
ne upar thi kudrat ni rehem chhe

Phaatela khissa ni aad maan muki chhe ame
chhalkaati malkaati mauj
Eklo ubhun ne toye mela maan houn
evun laagya kare chhe mane roj
Taalu vasaaye nahin evdi pataari maan
aapno khajaano hem-khem chhe

Aankhon maan paani to aave ne jaaye
nathi bheetar bheenaash thathi ochhi
Vadh ghat no kaanthaao raakhe hisaab
nathi parvaah samandar ne hoti
Sooraj to uge ane aathmiye jaaye
maari upar aakaash em-nem chhe

~

Your Ocean Is Full of Pearls / Ab Thaara Laal Samandada Ra

Ab thaara laal samandada ra maay
Ho marjeeva koi laal lyaave ho!

Marjeevon ka des ajab hai
Nugura thaag na paaya gura ji
Marjeeva ri gati sugura jaane
Ab ee nugura kayin bhurmaave?

Kaachi maati ka kumbh banaaya
Jin mein bhanvar lubhaaya gura ji
Jhoothi aa kaaya, jhoothi aa maaya
Ab ee jhootha ee dhandhe lagaaya

Aap taji ne baithi gaya samund mein
Motida se surat lagaaya gura ji
Heero heera laal padaarath lyaaya
Ab yo samundar chhodya nahin jaay

Har dam ka sauda kar le re bande
Soham taal bajaaya gura ji
Ratti ek svaansa hero ina ghat mein
Tab yeh pavan purush parkaashega

Nath Gulabi mhaane samrath mil gaya
Dhan guru mohe samjhaaya gura ji
Bhavani Nath sharan sadguru ki
Ab yo neki to saahibo nibhaave

~

Your Ocean Is Filled with Jewels / Thaara Bharya Samand Maan Heera

Thaara bharya samand maan heera,
marjeevala laaviya
Thaara ghat maanhi gyaan ka janjeera,
saahib suljhaaviya

Yo mann lobhi laalchi re
Yo mann kaalu keer
Bharam ki jaal chalaave re haan

Baagaan jo baagaan koyal bole
Ban maanhi bolya re rooda mor
Saavan vaali lehraan bhi aave re haan

Ghaas phoos sab jali gaya re
Rahi gayi saavan vaali Teej
Koi to din ulat aave re haan

Gola chhootya hai guru gyaan ka re
Kaayar bhaagyo re bhaagyo jaaye
Soorma sanmukh rehna re haan

Guru Ramanand ki fauj mein re
Sanmukh lade re Kabir
Shabad ka baan chalaaya re haan

~

Taste the Waves of the Ocean / Lai Le Samandara Ri Leher

Lai le samandara ri leher, mhaara veera re
Daabra doya se moti na mile, santon re bhai

Kya par tiriya se preet, mhaara veera re?
Jaise jeev ka kaal hai, santon re bhai

Kya pardesi se preet, mhaara veera re?
Jaise phoos ka taapna, santon re bhai

Mhaara guruji ki leeladi palhaani, mhaara veera re
Mamta ko jheen dharaaye
Mann tya bhukh mann taajna, santon re bhai

Dui kar jod Gorakh bole, mhaara veera re
Sat amraapur paaya hai, santon re bhai

~

My Boat Is Sailing Smoothly / Neeke Neeke Chaalan Laagi

Naiyya mori neeke neeke chaalan laagi
Aandhi megha, kachhu na vyaapai,
chadhe sant badbhaagi

Uthle reh to dar kachhu naahin
Naahin gehre ko sansa
Ulat jaay to baal na baanka
Ya hai ajab tamaasha

Ausar laage to parvat bojha
Taun na laage re bhaari
Dhan satguruji ne raah bataai
Ta ki re main balihaari

Kahe Kabira jo bin sir khevai
So yeh sumati bakhaane
Ya bahu hit ki akath katha hai
Birla khevat yeh jaane

14. THE ART OF DYING

The Beast of the Mind / Aapon Moner Baaghe

Aapon moner baaghe khaaye jaare
Kon khaane paalaale she jon baanchte paare?

Aami bondho chhondo kori ente
Phosh kore jaaye gire kete
Omnishe baagh gorjiye uthe
Aamaar mon paakhire de haana

Moraar aage jei morte paare
Taare kon baaghe ki korte paare
Mora she ki aabaar more?
Morile she amor hoye

Moraar aage jyante mora
Ae jeno guru shomudre
Mon jaahaaj ke nongor kora
Fakir Lalon bole mon potongo paara
Aagoon dekhe morte jaaye

~

Birth and Death / Jonomo Morono

Jonomo morono hobe nibaarono
Jodi koro mono morono shaadhona
Jonmile morono, morile jonomo
Jonomo morono, bheeshono jontrona

'Aa', 'u', 'ma', ei bedotroi
Mooladhaare swadhishthaane monipure roi
Shaadhonaaye shiddho jaaniho nischoy
Kaamini kanchone aashokti thaake na

Ida pingala, ei dui naadi
Hom shom jopichhe dibosho shorbori
Moddhe shushomna chokro bhed kori
Soham bhaabe hon she dwidole dolona

Tokhon shunite paaibe baanshiro lohori
Baajibe khol korotaal mridongo jhaanjhori
Shonkho ghonta koto baajibe obiroto
Bhomoro gunjone noopuro baajona

Shohostro dol komole Sri Radha Gobindo
Raasholeela kore shohochori shongo
Herile noyone paabi premanondo
Nirbaan muktiro shohojo shaadhona

~

The Bedroom of True Lovers (set of couplets)

Sir dhoondhiya dhad na lahaan, dhad dhoondhiya sir naahin
Hath karaayun aangiyun viya kapiji kaanhi
Vahdat je vihaaeen, je viya se vadhiya

Soori aahi seengaar, asal aashikan jo
Mudan motan meenhano, thiya nizaare nirvaar
Kusan jo karaar, asal aashikan khe

Kaati jin gare, maan lav laagi tin sein
Mahbat je maidaan mein, vanya per bhare
Adeea sir dhare, maan kuhniun supireen

~

Village of the Dead / Saadho Yeh Murdon Ka Gaon

Saadho yeh murdon ka gaon

Peer mare, paigambar mari hain,
Mari hain zinda jogi
Raaja mari hain, parja mari hain,
Mari hain baid aur rogi

Chanda mari hai, sooraj mari hai,
Mari hain dharni aakaasa
Chaudah bhavan ke chaudhari mari hain
Inhun ki ka aasa?

Nauhu mari hain, dasahu mari hain,
Mari hain sahaj atthaasi
Taintees koti devta mari hain,
Badi kaal ki baazi

Naam anaam anant rahat hai,
Dooja tattva na hoi
Kahe Kabir suno bhai saadho
Bhatak maro mat koi

~

Births and Deaths Become Easy / Sahaj Katega Chauraasi

Ant pe tant koi birla hi jaane bhaaya
Parde param guru aaya

Rat le bande alakh purush avinaashi
Banda thaari sahaj katega chauraasi
Thor bina to thikaano nahin laage bhaaya
Bina ho thika se thagai jaasi

Guru ke bina to phirunga bhatakto bhaaya
Bina ho guru ke pher jaasi

Naabhi kamal se uthi ek swaansa bhaaya
Dhan ho guruji thaari maaya

Doi kar jod jati Gorakh bole bhaaya
Saaheb Kabir poora khoji

15. THE BELOVED'S COUNTRY

Let's Go, My Sweet / Haalo Ni Mori Sajni

Haalo ni mori sajni
Jaaiye gura ji ra des
Piya ji vaala des

Nahin re uge nahin aathme
Nahin re pavan parves

Jab re jaagun rang mahal maan
Royi royi rudan karun

Hoon re sooti rang mahal maan
Royi royi rudan karun

Bhagva main rangaaun loogda
Leedho vairaagi vaalo ves

Chhodya re peehar, saasra
Chhodya saaheliya ro saath

Kabiro farmaave Dharmidas kun
Aa chhe mastaani vaalo khel

~

The Country of the Sky / Gagan Mandal Re Des

Haalo surta gagan mandal re des
Raaja to parja vahaan nahin pooge
Na pooge bhoop naresh

Kaal jaal jam vahaan nahin pooge
Pooge na dukh aur klesh

Brahma aur Vishnu jahaan nahin pooge
Na pooge shesh Mahesh

Ladu Nath kahe suno bhai Kisna
Aisa akhandi des

~

Such Amazing Signs / Evi Evi Sen

Evi evi sen bataai mhaane satguru
Mukh par kahyo nahin jaaye, re saadho

Hamaare re des maan na dhara nahin gagana
Nahin koi pavan nahin paani

Hamaare re des maan na chanda nahin sooraj
Nahin koi naulakh taara

Hamaare re des maan na Brahma nahin Vishnu
Nahin koi Shankar deva

Hamaare re des maan na Ved nahin Gita
Nahin koi shabad nahin saakhiya

Hamaare re des maan na uge nahin aathme
Nahin koi janme nahin mare

Manjale re manjale ek sant jai pahunchiya
Kabir sant chadhya nirvana

~

Such Is My Country / Aisa Des Hamaara

Mehram hove so ee lakh paave,
aisa des hamaara, haan

Ved kitaab paar nahin paaya,
kehnan sunan se nyaara, haan
Asht kamal nau das ke upar,
rehta purush hamaara, aisa des hamaara

Bin baadal ek dhaaman dhamke,
bin sooraj ujiyaara
Bina nain se maala poyi,
satt se shabad uchaara, aisa des hamaara

Sunn mahal mein baaja baaje,
kingri ben sitaara
Jo chadh dekhe gagan gufa mein,
darsega agam apaara, aisa des hamaara

Jal ki boond giri jal maanhi,
na meetha ne na khaara
Kahein Kabir suno bhai saadho,
koi pahunchega guru pyaara, aisa des hamaara

~

This Alien Country / Rehna Nahin Des Begaana Hai

Ab rehna nahin des begaana hai
Yahaan rehna nahin des veeraana hai
Begaana hai, yeh deewaana hai
Yahaan rehna nahin des begaana hai

Yeh sansaar kaagaz ki pudiya
Ise chhaant lage ghul jaana hai

Yeh sansaar kaanton ki bel hai
Yahaan ulajh pulajh mar jaana hai

Yeh sansaar phoos ki tapli
Ise taap lage jal jaana hai

Kahat Kabira suno re saadho
Aakhir sab ko jaana hai

~

City of Mirrors / Aarshinogor

Aachhe baareer kaachhe aarshinogor
Podoshi boshot kore
Taare dhori dhori mone kori
Dhora de na more
Ek jon podoshi boshot kore

Graam bediye agaadh paani
Taate naai toroni naai ko tori paare
O tui kemon kore paar jaabi
Bhoy dekhi ontore

Kebol boshei podosheer kotha
Jaar hosto podo skondho maatha naai re
Shetho khonek thaake shunnopore
Khonek bhaashe neere

Shei podoshi jodi aamaaye chhooto
Tobe jom jaatona doore jeto ek baare
Ae taai Shiraj Lalon ek shaathe roi
Lokho jojon doore

~

My Country's Boundless / Begam Des Hamaara

Gam na samre main nahin jaana
Revaan gam su main nyaara
Saadho bhai begam des hamaara

Dharti gam hai, aasmaan gam hai
Gam hai pavan aur paani

Chanda gam hai, sooraj gam hai
Gam hai nau lakh taara

Paandav gam hai, kerav gam hai
Gam hai das avataara

Shiv gam hai, shakti gam hai
Gam hai sakal sansaara

Machhandi prataap jati Gorakh bolya
Revo re gam su nyaara

~

Someone from My Land / Milo Re Milo

Arre bhai milo re milo koi mhaara des ra
Do do baataan karaanga ji
Arre bhai milya tha bolya nahin
Joona saadh kehvaana ji

Lakad lakad sab ek hai
Ek hi maalik ne gadhiya ji
Ek lakdi to dhooni mein jale
Doosri mahalaan mein jadiya ji

Patthar patthar sab ek hai
Una maalik ne ghadiya ji
Ek patthar ki moorat bani
Dooji peri mein gadhiyo ji

Dharti maata ra choolha kariya
Aasmaan kiya hai kadhela ji
Chaar jug jhonkan diya
Dhuaan gagan samaana ji

Doi kar jod Gorakh boliya
Paaya hai vaikunth vaasa ji
Jin ne ratiya sat naam ko
Voi nar pahuncha sat dhaam ji

~

It Rained Last Night / Raatab Meehada Vatha

Raatab meehada vatha
Khivdan khel kiya
Maadaanan je mulk mathe
Raatab meehada vatha

Kaara kakran kod kiya
Baadal boond vatha

Vathada meeh Maleer mein
Saava gha phuta

Chhibbad paka hin taliyan mein
Valiyan vel kiya

Maaru maal vathi achan
Kakkhan te the pakha

Utte unkdi aaiyaan
Sain sain soor satha

Adhiyun Shahu Latif chain
Sanghi subh khwaab mein ditha

~

Lightning Strikes (set of couplets)

Kismat kaid kaveeu, naat ker ache hin kot mein?
Aane likhiye loh je, handh dekhaaryum heeu
Parche keen panvhaar ree-a, jaani, juso aen jeeu
Raaja! Raazi theeu, ta Maarun mile Marui

Chiki, chikyam chaak, vanihyani vedichan ja
Vaajhaainde visaal khe, fanaa kayas firaak
Sei saaryam, Soomra! Thar janeeji thaak
Maaru-a je otaak, ghano ukandhi aahiyaan

Sanhee-a sui-a sibyo, yun Maaru-a sein saahu
Vethi saariyaan, Soomra! golaara aen gaahu
Hio muhinjo hut thiyo, hit mitti aen maahu
Pakhan manjh pasaahu, qaalib aahe kot mein

Vasi vijadiyan Umar udaasi kayo
Vatha meen Maleer tain saade mein sujan
Khivi khevadiyan badha mod Maleer khe

Khaab lahaanti Soomra chaank abaanan mein aaiyaan
Mitthi mak Maleer jo vethi veraaiyaan
Chhaila-chhailiyun paan mein kaam khayo kaaiyaan
Bheniyan manjhe chaank chibbad vaithi choondiyaan

Khaab lahaanti Soomra chaank vatan thi vanya
Dora dehaaiyan sain aaun bhitan paas bhanya
Aahe aas anya vatan vanyan ji Soomra

Kaiyam arz Allah ke piroh paand khani
Maaruda Maleer mein medindho mu dhani
Aahem ghurj ghani tin vahiyan vedichan ji

Sakhar sei deenham, je moon ghaarya band mein
Vasaaye vadfuda, mathe maadiyun meenham
Vaajhaaye visaal khe, thiyas tahivaarun tee-am
Neer muhinje neenham, ujaare achho kayo

16. SONGS OF FULFILMENT

Words of Truth / Satt Re Vachan

Satt re vachan saadhu ko bhar bhariya, ho ji
Bhariya hai taaram taar
Naam ro piyaalo saadho nirbhay thi peeyo, ho ji
Paayo mhaare satguru ae aaj
Surta chadhi saadhu aasmaan maan, ho ji

Bhanvar gufa maan dhani mhaaro baithiya, ho ji
Bhanvara kari le gunjaar
Unmuni aasan saadhu sevta, ho ji
Bhari rahiya hai bharpoor

Vina re vaadadiye veejo khave rahiyo, ho ji
Anhad varse hai noor

Kheem re khaada vinya nar joojhe, ho ji
Bhaan guru ae bataayo hai bhed

~

Soak up the Sky-Nectar / Peele Ameeras Dhara

Tu peele ameeras dhaara,
gagan mein jhadi lagi
Jhadi lagi haan jhadi lagi

Boond ka pyaasa ghada bhar paaya,
sapne mein vo swaad na aaya
Kaho kise kaise samjhaayein,
ek boond ki taran lagi

Pyaas bina kya peeve re paani,
pyaase ke liye vo paani
Bin adhikaar koi nahin jaani,
amrit ras ki jhadi lagi

Ameeras peeve amar pad paave,
bhav yoni mein kabahun nahin aave
Janam maran ka dukh nasaave,
ghat ki gagariya bharan lagi

Boond ameeras guruji ki baani,
jeevan rasta hai yeh paani
Kabir sangat mein ho hamaari,
daali prem ki hari bhari

~

My Heart's on Its Feet / Naachu Re Mero Mann

Naachu re mero mann nat hoye
Gyaan ke dhol bajaaye rain din
Sabd sune sab koi
Raahu Ketu navgrah naache
Jampur anand hoi

Chhaapa tilak lagaaye baans chadhi
Hoi rahu jag se nyaara
Sahas kala kar mann mero naache
Reejhe sirjanhaara

Jo tum kood jaao bhavsaagar
Kala badaaun mein tero
Kahe Kabir, suno bhai saadho
Ho rahu satguru chero

~

My Mind Has Taken to Living Free / Mann Laago Fakiri Mein

Mann laago mero yaar fakiri mein
Mann laago mero yaar garibi mein

Jo sukh paavega naam bhajan mein
Vo sukh naahin re ameeri mein

Haath mein tumba bagal mein sota
Chaaron disha jaageeri mein

Bhala bura sab ka sun leeje
Kar guzraan garibi mein

Prem nagar mein rehni hamaari
Bhali bani aayi saboori mein

Aakhir yeh tan khaak milega
Kaahe phirat magroori mein?

Kahein Kabir suno bhai saadho
Saahib milega saboori mein

~

I'm Drunk on Joy / Mann Mast Hua

Mann mast hua phir kya bole?

Heera paaya baandh gathadiya
Baar baar va ko kyon khole?

Halki thi jab chadhi taraaju
Poori bhayi phir kya tole?

Surat kalaalan bhayi matvaali
Madva pi gayi antole

Hansa nhaave Mansarovar
Taal talaiya mein kyon dole?

Kahein Kabir, suno bhai saadho
Saahib mil gaya til ole

~

Sweep the Path Clear / Maragiya Buhaarun

Maaragiya buhaarun, phulada bichhaaun
Krishan ji ra darshan paaya Hari Raam

Papaiyo hoi, aabhe maan baithi
Aabhe ri ghor suhaai Hari Raam

Bhamro hoi, phulada maan baithi
Phulada ri sugandh suhaai Hari Raam

Koyal hoi, baagaan maan baithi
Baagaan ri khushbu suhaai Hari Raam

Bolya Bai Meera, Girdhar gaayo
Charnaan maan sheesh namaayo Hari Raam

~

Crow, Sing Sweetly / Madhur Sur Bol Re Kaaga

Madhur sur bol re kaaga
Meera ro mann Raam se laaga

Piya ji thaaro panth hai bhaari
Mujhe prem ki kataari daari

Piya ji thaare baag mein jaati
Phoolon ri bhar chhaabadi laati

Piya ji thaaro mukhdo joti
Nit uth prem se dhoti

Piya ji thaare haath mein haldi
Meera bhayi paan se jaldi

Piya ji ra jas Meera gaave
Piya mhaare hirday bas aave

~

No Sun, No Moon / Bina Chanda Bina Bhaan

Bina chanda re bina bhaan,
sooraj bina hoya ujiyaala re
Parloka mat jaao,
parakh le yahin uniyaaro re

Arre heli mhaari!
Goonga gaave hai abe raag,
behro sunva laago hai
Paangaliyo naache re ghano naach,
aandhadiyo narkhan laago hai

Arre heli mhaari!
Gagan mandal ke beech,
tape koi jogi matvaalo hai
Nahin agan vaan babhoot,
nahin re koi taapan vaalo hai

Arre heli mhaari!
Shoonya shikhar ke beech,
macho ek jhagdo bhaari hai
Nahin kaayar ko yaan kaam,
kaayar ko kain patiyaaro hai?

Arre heli mhaari!
Gaave Gulabi Das,
khulya mhaara hirday ra taala hai
Bolya Bhavani Nath,
hoya mhaara ghat ujiyaala hai

~

In This Body / Ya Ghat Bheetar

Ya ghat bheetar baag bageeche
Ya hi mein sirjanhaara
Dhoondhe re dhoondhe andhiyaara

Ya ghat bheetar saat samandar
Ya hi mein nau lakh taara

Ya ghat bheetar heera aur moti
Ya hi mein parkhanhaara

Ya ghat bheetar anhad garje
Ya hi mein uthat phuvaara

Kahe Kabira, suno bhai saadho
Ya hi mein guru hai hamaara

~

Sun-Gourd, Moon-String / Sooja Lao Sassi

Sooja laao saasi laageli taanti
Anaaha daandi eki kiyata avadhooti
Sooja laao saasi

Baajai ala saahi herua beena
Suna taanti dhwani bilasayi roona

Aali kaaliye beni saari suniya
Gauwaara samarasa saandhi guniya

Jabe karaha karaha kaale chaapiyu
Bateesa taanti dhwani sa-ala biyaapiyu
Naachanti bajeela gaanti devi
Buddha naataka beesama hoi

~

O, She Really Wooed Him / Ghano Rijhaayo

Yo var paayo vo laadli ne
Yo var paayo ji
Ghano rijhaayo vo baanwari ne
Ghano rijhaayo ji
Mhaari surat suhaagan naval bani
Saahib var paayo ri

Bhatkat bhatkat sab jug bhatkya
Aaj ko avsar aayo heli
Ab ka avsar chook jaaoga
Phir nahin thikaana paaya

Prem ki peethi surat ki haldi
Naam ko tel chadhaayo heli
Paanch sakhi mil mangal gaave
Motiya mandap chhaayo

Sat naam ki chanwari rachaai
Padlo prem savaayo heli
Avinaashi ka jodya hathela
Brahma lagan lagaayo

Rang mahal mein sej piya ki
Odhe surat savaayo heli
Ab mhaari preet piya sang laagi
Jab sab santan mil paayo

Chauraasi ka phera phar kar
Bind paran ghar aayo heli
Kahein Kabir suno bhai saadho
Yo hans badhaavo gaayo

~

From the House of Farid / Ganj-e-Shakar

Ganj-e-shakar more Baba ke dar se
Banada bane chale Gesu Daraz
Ghar ghar jaage ri baaje badhaava
Beech sitaaron jo chale maahtaab

Kaisan kaisan aaye ri baaraati
Mangal dharat aakaash diya baati
Sehra laaye Ali maharaaj
Aage khade hain Garib Nawaz

Hujveri daata rahe muskaaye
Peeraan peer Geelani bhi aaye
Shamsi Rumi aaye bhi saath
Kaisi utri naghmon ki raat

Jangam jogi naath Kabira
Baaje mridang dhol manjeera
Nanak Shah aaye fakira
Anhad baaje har su aaj

~

I Have Given up Myself / Vaari Jaaun Re

Main vaari jaaun re, balihaari jaaun re
Mera satguru aangan aaya, main vaari jaaun re

Satguru aangan aaya, Ganga Gomti nhaaya
Meri nirmal ho gayi kaaya

Sab sakhi mil kar haalo, kesar tilak lagaavo
Ghane het su levo badhaai

Satguru darshan deenha, bhaag uday hi keenha
Mera dharam (karam) bharam sab chheena

Satsang ban gayi bhaari, mangala gaaun chaari
Meri khuli hriday ki baari

Das Narayan jas gaayo, charanon mein sees nimaayo
Mera satguru paar utaare

17. SONGS OF PRAISE

Praise, O Creator / Dhanya Teri Kartaar

Dhanya teri kartaar kala ka
Paar nahin koi paata hai

Niraakaar bhi hokar swaami
Sab ka tu paalan karta hai
Niraakaar nirbandhan swaami
Janam maran nahin dharta hai

Teri satta ka khel niraala
Birla hi mehram paata hai
Jin par kripa bhayi nij teri
Tu va ko daras dikhaata hai

Rishi muni aur sant mahaatma
Nis din dhyaan lagaata hai
Chaar khaan chauraasi ke maanhi
Tu hi nazar ek aata hai

Patte patte par roshni teri
Bijli si chamak dikhaata hai
Chakit bhaya mann buddhi teri
Jeeva Das gun gaata hai

~

No Measure of Your Greatness / Ant Bahar Di

Ant bahar di, kal na kaain
Rangi rang banaaya
Allah aadmi ban aaya
Maula aadmi ban aaya

Na main mangi, na main parni
Jholi baal jhulaaya
Ujar kitta val daane khaavan da
Beheston aap tadaaya

Haabil Kaabil putt aadam de
Aadam kis da jaaya?
Assaan Aadam Khan nu agge hoya sun
Aadam saadda jaaya

Aan baazigar baazi patedi
Putla jod banaaya
Gali gali vich dhol vajaaunda
Naachu ishq nachaaya

Ain di chaadar, Meem da burkha
Mukh pe ghoonghat paaya
Ali Raza hai naam hamaara
Bulleya naam daraaya

~

You Are My Love / Menda Ishq Bhi Tu

Tu bas tu
Hey maula
Tu bas tu
Bas tu tu tu
Bas tu

Tu dil mein to aata hai
Samajh mein nahin aata
Bas jaan gaya main
Teri pehchaan yahi hai

Mera ishq bhi tu, mera yaar bhi tu
Menda deen bhi tu, eemaan bhi tu
Menda kaaba qibla masjid mimbar
Mushaf te Qur'an bhi tu

Menda jism vi tu, meri rooh vi tu
Menda kalb vi tu, ji jaan vi tu
Menda zikr vi tu, menda fikr vi tu
Mera zauk bhi tu, vajdaan bhi tu

~

Dancing to His Tune / Kaisa Naach Nachaaya

Aadmi ban aaya re dhola
Kaisa naach nachaaya

Apni godi aap hi khele
Ban kar Mohan laala
Aap hi bove, aap hi seenche
Aap phire rakhvaala, dhola

Aap hi bhatti, aap hi madghar
Aap hi hot kalaala
Aap hi peeve aap pilaave
Aap phire matvaala, dhola

Haabil Kaabil Aadam ke jaaye
Kaho Aadam kiska jaaya?
Daal Khaleel ko naar ke andar
Aap hi shor machaaya, dhola

18. ISHQ / LOVE

The Tale of Love's Amazement / Khabar-e-Tahayyur-e-Ishq Sun

Khabar-e-tahayyur-e-ishq sun
Na junoon raha na pari rahi
Na to tu raha, na to main raha
Jo rahi so bekhabari rahi

Vo ajab ghadi thi ke jis ghadi
Liya dars nuskha-e-ishq mein
Ke kitaab aql ki taaq par
Jo dhari thi yun hi dhari rahi

Chali samt-e-gaib se ik hawa
Ke chaman suroor ka jal gaya
Magar ek shaakh-e-nihaal-e-gam
Jise dil kahein so hari rahi

Kiya khaak aatish-e-ishq ne
Dil-e-be-nava-e-Siraj ko
Na khatar raha na hazar raha
Magar ek bekhatari rahi

~

Drunk on Love / Haman Hain Ishq Mastaana

Haman hain ishq mastaana,
haman ko hoshiyaari kya?
Rahein aazaad ya jag mein,
haman duniya se yaari kya?

Jo bichhude hain piyaare se,
bhatakte dar badar phirte
Hamaara yaar hai ham mein,
haman ko intezaari kya?

Na pal bichhude piya hamse,
na ham bichhude piyaare se
Unhin se neh laagi hai,
haman ko beqaraari kya?

Kabira ishq ka maata,
dui ko door kar dil se
Jo chalna raah naazuk hai,
haman sir bojh bhaari kya?

~

My Beloved Has Come Home / Mera Piya Ghar Aaya

Mera piya ghar aaya, ho laal ji
Ghadiyaali devo nikaal ni
Piya ghar aaya, saannu Allah milaaya
Hun hoya fazal kamaal ni

Ghadi ghadi ghadiyaal bajaave
Rain vasal di paya ghataave
Mere mann di baat je paave
Hatthon ja sutte ghadiyaal ni

Anhad vaaja vaje shahaana
Mutrib sughda taal taraana
Bhul gaya vazu namaaz dogaana
Mad pyaala de hun kalaal ji

Mukh vekhan da ajab nazaara
Dukh dile da mit gaya saara
Rain vadhe kuchh karo pasaara
Din agge dharo hun deewaal ni

Bullehshah di sej niyaari
Ni main taaranhaare taari
Kivein Kivein hun aayi vaari
Hun vichhadan hoya muhaal ni

~

The River of Love (set of couplets)

Khusro rain suhaag ki
jo main jaagi pi ke sang
Tan mera mann preetam ka
so do bhaye ek hi rang

Khusro baazi prem ki
jo main kheli pi ke sang
Jeet gayi to piya more
haari to main pi ke sang

Khusro nadiya prem ki
ulti va ki dhaar
Jo ubhra so doob gaya
jo dooba so paar

~

Be True to My Love / Aisi Mhaari Preet Nibhaavjo

Aisi mhaari preet nibhaavjo
Ho nirdhan ka ho Raam
Ho durbal ka ho Raam
Bhavsaagar mein bhoolo mati

Tam to jharkat ham beladi
Raanga tam se liptaaye
Tam to dhalado ne ham sookhi jaavaan
Mhaara kai ho havaal?

Tam to samdar ham maachhli
Raanga tamaara ho maaye
Tam to sookho ne ham mari jaavaan
Mhaara kai ho havaal?

Tam to baadal ham moriya
Raanga tam se harkhaaye
Raanga tam se judaaye
Tam to garjo ne ham boliya
Tam to barso ne ham boliya
Mhaara kai ho havaal?

Kahein ho Kabir Dharmidas se,
piyu thaara ghat maaye
Kahein ho Kabir Dharmidas se,
piyu hirday dhadakaaye

~

Love Stripped Me / Ishq De Mahakme

Ik din gaya main ishq de mahakme
Ishq ne meri vaddaai lut li
Main to gayo ishq di daad lene
Ishq ne meri dhaanaai lut li
Ishq peer paigambaraan nu lut lehenda
Vadde vaadshaah di vaadshaahi lut li
Ae naadaan Bulleya,
ishq ne tera ki lutteya?
Ishq ne to khuda ki khudaai lut li

~

Come into My Eyes (set of couplets)

Saajan phool gulaab ro,
to main phoolaan ri baas
Saajan mhaaro kaaljo,
to main saajan ro saans

Saajan main tore thaan ki,
aur basun veeraane vaas
Kaam karun ghar aapro,
par jivdo tameere paas

Preetam ke pattiyaan likhun
jo vo base vides
Tan mein mann mein nainan mein,
ta ko kaun sandes?

Nainaan antar aav tu,
naina jhanp tohe lun
Na main dekhun aur ko,
na tohe dekhan dun

~

I Saw Myself / Dekha Apne Aap Ko

Dekha apne aap ko,
mera dil deewaana ho gaya
Na chhedo yaaron mujhe,
main khud masti mein aa gaya

Laakhon sooraj chandrama
qurbaan hain mere husn par
Adbhut chhavi ko dekh ke,
kehne se main sharma gaya

Ab khudi se baahir hain hum,
ishq kafni pehen kar
Sab rang mein chola ranga,
deedaar apna ho gaya

Ab deekhta koi nahin,
duniya mein hi mere siva
Doori ka parda hata,
saara bharam vinya gaya

Achal Ram ab khud ba khud,
hai mehboob mujh se na juda
Nij noor mein bharpoor ho,
apne mein aap sama gaya

BRIEF BIOGRAPHIES OF SELECTED POETS*

Amir Khusro Dehlavi (1253–1325), known as Tuti-e-Hind (Parrot of India), was a scholar, musician and a great poet belonging to the Chishti order of Sufis. He is often credited with the beginnings of the languages that we now understand as modern day Hindi and Urdu, which both evolved from 'Hindavi'—a mélange of languages like Bhojpuri and Persian—in which Khusro composed several of his popular works. Brij Bhasha, Arabic and Sanskrit too are part of his body of work. He was a court poet of several rulers of Delhi Sultanate, but was also a close disciple of Nizamuddin Auliya—the great Chishti Sufi of Delhi. His poems reflect the social and cultural life of Delhi of those times in great detail. He is credited with having created the 'qawwali'—a form of Sufi devotional music—by blending the traditions of Persian and Hindustani classical music.

Bhavani Nath or Bhavani Das was a saint-poet of the Bhakti tradition from Gujarat, believed to have been born in 1775 into the Vankar community in Dholka village. Though in the signature line of his songs, he invokes his guru as Gulabi Nath, according to some sources perhaps his guru was Jodha Bhakt.

Bhusuku, also known as Shantideva, was most likely a Buddhist Siddha, a Mahayana poet and philosopher, who lived somewhere around the 8th century. He was born as Prince Shantivarman, son of the King of Saurashtra, but he gave up the royal life to follow a spiritual path. He became a disciple of Jayadeva at Nalanda, where he was ordained into the Madhyamika order. At this monastery Shantivarman received his two

---

*Drafted and/or compiled by Prashant Parvatneni and other team members at the Kabir Project, Bengaluru. We have no information about several of the poets in the book, and so their biographies are not featured here. For further references, please visit www.ajabshahar.com/people/all.

popular names—Bhusuku and Shantideva. He was called 'Bhusuku—The Idler' because he seems to have been interested in just three things—eating (bhu), sleeping (su), and strolling (ku): hence Bhusuku. However, he is believed to have mastered knowledge of the scriptures through intense meditation on his favourite deity, Manjushri. Later during his journeys, he became a 'Raut' (a military personnel) at the court of the King of Madhyadesha. He then travelled to Bengal and married a Chandali woman, where he is very popular among seekers, especially the Bauls.

Brahmanand was a saint and a poet from Pushkar, Rajasthan. He is considered to be the first saint of the Mauji Ram Satsang Sabha. He is often confused with Brahmanand Swami who was a leading exponent of the Swaminarayan Sampradaya. These two figures from Rajasthan however have their own body of works which differ in terms of language, style and thematic concerns.

Bulleshah (c. 1680–1758) is among the most beloved Sufi poets of Punjab who left an indelible mark on the ethos of Punjab and the cultural fabric of the sub-continent. He was born Sayyad Muhammad Abdullah Shah into a family believed to be direct descendants of the Prophet Muhammad, whose ancestors had migrated to Punjab from Iraq. However, as he grew up he dropped the title and called himself Bulleshah or simply 'Bullah'—the way his mother would address him. His spiritual quest took him to the house of a gardener in Kasur, Shah Inayat Qadiri, the great Sufi murshid who taught both Bulleshah and Waris Shah. Bulleshah wrote poetry in Punjabi and Saraiki (a dialect of Punjabi) primarily in the form of kaafis.

Dev Dungarpuri is a 19th-century saint-poet from Rajasthan, believed to have been born in 1794 in Marwad. He wrote in Hindi, Gujarati and Marwadi languages and is said to have been a disciple of Bhavpuri. Of his birth and early life, there are two different versions. According to one, he was born a brahmin and later become a priest at an ashram in Jaisalmer. Another legend says that he was born into the vankar caste to parents—Bhavji Bhagat and Rudi Ba—in Detroj village in Gujarat. There is however an agreement over his final days, which he spent in Ameergadh village in Palampur taluka of Gujarat, where he is reputed to have taken samaadhi.

Dharamdas (c. 1433-1543) is considered to be one of earliest disciples of the 15th-century nirgun Bhakti poet Kabir, and songs bearing his signature are widely prevalent in the oral traditions of Kabir in central and western India. He is held to be the founder of the Dharamdasi sect of the Kabir Panth, with its headquarters in Chhattisgarh. Born to a wealthy family, he grew up to be a rich and devout businessman known as Dhani Dharamdas. Legend says that during one of his travels he met Kabir in Varanasi, who introduced him to the nirgun tradition of divinity beyond form. The fact that many songs of Kabir flowing in the oral traditions carry the signature line, 'Kabir says to Dharamdas', is for the Dharamdasi Kabir Panthis evidence of Dharamdas's closeness to Kabir. As a saint-poet, Dharamdas's poems are widely sung in the villages of Bihar, Chhattisgarh, Madhya Pradesh, Rajasthan and Gujarat.

Dhruv Bhatt (born 1947) is a contemporary Gujarati novelist and poet, based in Karamsad, Gujarat. He has received numerous awards for his works, including the prestigious Sahitya Akademi award in 2002 for his novel *Tattvamasi*. He has worked closely with children and a lot of his works draw heavily from nature, particularly his poetry. He is deeply interested in the nature of faith in India.

Gorakhnath, also known as Gorakshanath, or simply Gorakh, is a legendary figure, who is said to have lived roughly around the 11th or 12th century. He was a disciple of Matsyendranath (or Machhindernath) who is said to be the founder of the Nath Sampradaya, an ascetic tradition closely associated with the practice of Hatha yoga. Through Gorakh's songs and yogic teachings, the Nath sect gained immense popularity. There are many legends, temples and iconic caves where he is believed to have meditated and even a whole city that takes its name from him—Gorakhpur. Though Gorakhpur has been in news recently for acute communal polarisation, it used to be famous for the widespread following the Nath sect had among Muslims. There are still many Muslim yogis who wear saffron robes, play the sarangi and sing Gorakh's bhajans. Many believe that Gorakh was crucial to the development of a syncretic Bhakti tradition which gained both credence and popularity among common folk through his songs. The influence of Gorakh is seen on several Bhakti poets and saints who came after him, especially Kabir—the vocabulary of Hatha Yoga, for example. Gorakh also made popular the 'twilight language' (sandhya bhasha) of the tantric traditions—utterances which were coded, deliberately ambiguous and enigmatic.

Hamsa (Parvathy Baul) is a Baul singer and practitioner, painter and storyteller from Bengal who has been a disciple of Shashanko Goshai and

Sanatan Das Baul. A leading proponent of Baul philosophy and music, Parvathy's journey started with the more classical forms of art. Born into a Bengali brahmin family, Parvathy learnt Hindustani music and Kathak early on in life. She went on to study visual art at Shantiniketan. Once while on a train to Shantiniketan, Parvathy heard a blind Baul singer singing the songs of the mystics. She was immediately struck by the music and went to Phulmala Baul, a regular at Shantiniketan to learn this music. She received her initiation into Baul practice from Sanatan Das Baul, her first true guru. She is currently engaged in creating a Baul gurukul for the learning of Baul practice and songs.

Kabir is arguably the most popular and influential mystic poet of India, who is believed to have lived in the town of Varanasi in north India in the 15th century. Kabir was probably born to a couple who were weavers by profession (julahas) and his ancestors were recent converts to Islam, though popular legend tends to ascribe his birth to a brahmin widow who subsequently abandoned him. Kabir grew up to be a weaver and was possibly married with children. He spoke not in the language of scholars but in the common parlance of the folk. He was likely illiterate, and often refers to his low-caste status. Kabir is one of the most iconic figures of the Bhakti movement which brought about a profound shift in spiritual practice, seeking to forge a deeper, more intimate relationship with the divine.

Kheem Saheb (c. 1734–1801) is a Bhakti saint-poet belonging to the Ravi Bhaan Sampradaya—a sect of the Kabir Panth popular in the Saurashtra region of Gujarat. Born into the Lohana caste, Kheem was initiated into this path by his father and guru Ravi Bhaan himself, later dedicating his life to propagating the Ravi Bhaan Sampradaya in the Kutch region of Gujarat. The songs and poetry of Kheem Saheb take the forms of bhajan, kaafi, garbi and aarti expressing ideas of the nirgun path, importance of the guru, the spiritual practice of Yoga and the theme of vairagya (renunciation and asceticism). Written in the common man's dialect of Sadhukkadi Hindi, one of Kheem Saheb's most famous works is *Chintamani* (1770). He also wrote in Kutchi and Gujarati dialects. Maluk Das and the famous Dalit saint-poet Trikham Saheb were his prominent disciples who carried his legacy forward.

Khwaja Ghulam Farid (1845–1901) was a Punjabi / Saraiki Sufi poet. He lived and died in Chachran Sharif in present-day Pakistan, and was buried in Kot Mithan. He lost his mother while he was only four or five years old, and his father died when he was twelve. He subsequently passed under the tutelage of his elder brother. He spoke and wrote in several languages, including Persian. His verse is in the form of kaafi and dohade (couplets).

Lalon Fakir (c. 1772–1890) was a Baul singer and poet, widely regarded as a great social reformer of his time. Lalon's poetry reveals imprints from a number of spiritual philosophies—Islam, Buddhism, Jainism, Tantrism and Hindu Vaishnavism. He may have been born into a family of Hindu Kayasthas in a small village in present-day Bangladesh. The story goes that while on a pilgrimage with some fellow villagers, Lalon contracted smallpox, and was left for dead on the banks of the Ganga. There, he was found by a weaver couple from a largely Muslim village called Cheuriya, who were possibly responsible for the Islamic influences on his life and works. Lalon set up an akhada (a space for spiritual / music practice) with their help and started composing and singing songs. Lalon's poetry, while being deeply spiritual, is also a sharp social commentary against sectarianism on the basis of caste, religion and race. He is known to have been a major influence on the works of Rabindranath Tagore. Allen Ginsberg, a Beat poet of USA, was also heavily influenced by him and wrote a poem in his memory titled 'After Lalon'.

Madan Gopal Singh is a renowned Sufi singer who composes and interprets the poetry of Sultan Bahu, Shah Hussain, Baba Farid, Kabir and Bulleh Shah among others. Himself a poet and translator, he effortlessly blends his original compositions with verses of mystic poets and translations of poets as disparate as Bertolt Brecht and John Lennon while singing. His father Harbhajan Singh was a noted Punjabi poet, and Madan Gopal's childhood was steeped in literature and culture. Starting off with popular Bollywood numbers, he picked up singing on his own and till date he has never had a guru or an ustaad. Today, he performs extensively with his ensemble 'Chaar Yaar' (Four Friends). Apart from being an artist and practitioner, Madan Gopal Singh is also a thinker and scholar who writes about cinema, art and culture.

Meera Bai (16th century) is one of the most popular and well-known saint-poets to have emerged from the Bhakti tradition. Her bhajans, composed in the form of metrical lyrics or padas, are widely sung across diverse languages and cultures of the subcontinent. Unlike nirgun saints,

Meera's devotion was singularly focused on the image of a popular deity of the Hindu traditions—Krishna. Born into a Rajput family, she was married against her will to Raja Bhoj Raj of Mewar who died very soon after in battle. Meera never took to royal life and preferred to roam the streets like a yogini, singing to Krishna. Her behaviour was considered unacceptable, and she was continually persecuted by her family of marriage, especially her brother-in-law and subsequent King, Vikram Singh. Stories of her miraculous escapes from various attempts to murder her abound in legends around her life.

Nanak Das (not to be confused with Guru Nanak, the first Sikh guru) was a Bhakti poet who belonged to the Ravi-Bhaan Sampradaya—a stream of the Kabir Panth with a large following in the Gujarat-Saurashtra region. Born to Krishna Das in the Garu community of Diksar village in Surendranangar, Gujarat, he was a disciple of Gang Saheb. According to legend he lived for over a hundred years from 1794 to 1901, writing over 300 devotional songs during his lifetime.

Narayan Das was a Bhakti saint-poet of the 19th century who was born in Madakla village in Gujarat. His parents passed away when he was very young and he grew up under the care of his uncle. He moved to Kanesra village when he was twenty years old, later establishing a Ramji temple there. His bhajans are compiled in the Narayan Bhajan Sagar. Lal Das is believed to be his guru, though in many of his bhajans, saints like Moti Das and Ugam are also referred to as his gurus.

Panju Shah (c. 1851–1914) was a mystic poet from Bengal, born in a village called Jenaidah. It was after his strict father's death that Shah started learning Baul songs from his guru Hirajtullah Khandakar. Shah composed over 400 songs which reflected the diversity of styles and ideas prevalent in the syncretic culture of undivided Bengal. His songs blended Baul tunes with those of kirtan and jari gaan; some were compiled into a collection called *Sohi Eski Sadeki Gauhor*. It is believed that Shah had met the iconic Lalon Fakir and the encounter left a deep impression on him. Like Lalon, Shah too established an akhada for Baul seekers to practice and share songs and ideas. Fikir Shah, Rais Shah and Matam Shah were some of Panju Shah's disciples.

Rohal Fakir (c. 1734–1804), also known as the 'Kabir of Sindh', was a Sufi mystic poet who was deeply interested in Hindu philosophy. He wrote poetry in Sindhi, but also in Hindi, Saraiki, Dhakti and Marwadi. His poetry is a wonderful coming together of Sufi mysticism and devotional Bhakti. *Man Parbodh*, *Udhbhit Granth*, *Surab Giyan* and *Agham Warta* are four of his most important works. He has also written Krishna padas, aartis and holis. He was born in a village called Padma Bhit in Sindh into the zangeja caste of Shia Muslims. Rohal was made the minister of the royal treasury when his father, an important member of the royal court, passed away. His next appointment was to be an ambassador for the court, opening up avenues of travel and cultural exchange. He had already been initiated into the spiritual path by Sufi Izatullah Shah Sufi-ul-Qadri at Jhok Sharif where he had performed rigorous meditations in isolation. As a practicing Sufi and a political ambassador, Rohal played an important role in building a syncretic culture of sharing spiritual knowledge and ideas.

Sachal Sarmast (c. 1739–1829) was a Sufi poet of Sindh whose unfettered poetry attacked religious orthodoxy and professed faith in the Oneness of Being. Known as 'the poet in seven languages', he wrote in Sindhi, Saraiki, Persian, Arabic, Baluchi, Punjabi and Urdu. Born as Abdul Wahhab in the village of Daraza to a wealthy family, his father died soon after his birth, and he was raised by his uncle Abdul Haqq. Haqq became his spiritual guide, opening up the world of Sufism, Islam and Sindhi lore. He earned the name 'Sachal' ('the truthful one') from Shah Latif. As his poetic pseudonym Sachal adopted the name 'Sarmast' ('intoxicated') to evoke his immersion and oneness with god. The other pseudonym used for his Persian poems was 'Ashikar' (meaning 'open'). Sachal knew the Qur'an inside out and was deeply influenced by the Persian poetry of Attar and Hafez. Sarmast married at a young age and lost his wife within two years, after which he chose to remain unattached and generally preferred a solitary way of life.

Shah Abdul Latif lived from 1689 to 1752 CE, writing most of his poetry in the first half of the 18th century. Latif is widely held to be the greatest poet of the Sindhi language. Most of his poetry was collected into a single work now referred to as *Shah Jo Risalo* ('Risalo' means 'treatise' or 'message'), best remembered for its seven tragic romances which include Sasui-Punhu, Sohini-Mehar and Umar-Marui, among others. Latif was born in a village called Hala Haveli in Sindh in a prominent Sayyad family (held to be descendants of Prophet Muhammad himself). He is reputed to have been well-versed in the Qur'an and the Hadiths, and the poetry of Rumi as well as his great grandfather, Shah Abdul Karim Bulri. Disappointed in love when his beloved's father refused his proposal, Latif is said to have left home and wandered for three years with Nath Panthi yogis. Later he was able to marry the woman he loved, but she died soon after. His life was spent mostly in contemplation and music, and he acquired a certain following as a saint. Against the rigid rules of the Islamic preachers, Shah Latif was a practitioner of music. He is believed to have invented a poetic verse form, which is also a style of singing known as waai, and also a stringed instrument called the dhambura—a variation of the tambura—which continues to be played by folk singers.

Shashanko Goshai is a Baul singer and practitioner, also guru to the singer Parvathy Baul. Shashanko was born in a Vaishnav household in Shingar village of Murshidabad. Shashanko lost his father, a percussionist, when he was only thirteen. He earned money by working in a sweet shop and playing female roles in a Jatra (musical folk theatre form of Bengal) company, becoming quite famous as an actor. However, it was the devastating famine of 1943 that made Shashanko Ghoshai turn to the mystical path of Baul. He repaired his father's old ektara and started singing Baul songs. After a few years of practice, he was initiated into the tradition by Nityanando Goshai. Many remember Shashanko Goshai as a strict and reticent Baul master who continued to practice Baul in the old way, with only an ektara and duggi as accompaniments, rarely using other instruments such as the smaller dupki.

Siraj Aurangabadi (c. 1715–1763) was a Sufi poet from Aurangabad, Maharashtra. Born Syed Sirajuddin, Siraj started composing poetry first in Persian and then in Urdu. He was majorly influenced by Hafez. He wrote primarily in the Ghazal form, but also wrote long narrative verses. He was a practising Sufi and is said to have withdrawn from social life in his later years.

INDIVIDUAL TRANSLATION CREDITS

Poems translated by Vipul Rikhi

Page numbers: 4, 7, 8, 9, 10 • 14, 15, 15, 16, 17, 20 • 27, 28, 28, 30, 31, 32, 33 • 40, 41, 42, 46, 47, 48, 52, 53 • 56, 57, 59, 60, 61, 62 • 67, 68, 69 (HFYB) • 76, 76, 78, 79, 79, 80 • 85, 87 • 92, 92, 94, 95 • 100, 101, 103, 104, 104 • 110, 111 (TGuMG), 115, 117, 118, 118 • 122, 123, 124, 125, 126, 127 • 131, 132, 134, 135 • 139, 140, 141, 143 • 148, (TCotS), 149, 150, 151, 152, 153 • 161, 162, 165, 166, 168, 169, 171, 172 • 176, 177, 178, 179 • 181, 182, 183, 184, 185, 186, 186 •

Poems translated by Shabnam Virmani

Page numbers: 5 • 19, 22 • 44, 45, 49, 51 • 82 • 133 • 142 • 170 •

Poems translated by Shabnam Virmani and Vipul Rikhi

Page numbers: 18, 21 • 29, 34, 35 • 50 • 58 • 69 (TDCW), 70, 71 • 75, 81 • 86 • 96 • 102, 105 • 111 (NGLtG), 112, 113, 114 • 147, 148 (SAS), 154, 155 • 160, 163, 164, 167 • 187 •

NOTES

1. Ajab Shahar—Kabir Project. "'There are multiple Kabirs challenging the literary canon," says Apoorvanand.' September 2016. YouTube video, 12:54. https://youtu.be/t7a24_EJI6U. Accessed on 3 July 2019.
2. Stephen Mitchell (trans.), *Tao Te Ching* (New York: Harper Perennial Modern Classics, 2006), Verse 36.
3. See, for instance, P.D. Ouspensky, *In Search of the Miraculous: Fragments of an Unknown Teaching* (Orlando: Harvest / HBJ, 1977), 77.
4. Coleman Barks (trans.), *The Essential Rumi* (New Jersey: Castle Books, 1997), 36.
5. Sri Aurobindo, *Thoughts and Aphorisms* (Pondicherry: Sri Aurobindo Ashram Publication Department, 1958), 'Jnana', Aphorism 6.
6. John 1:1
7. Hebrews 4:12
8. Eknath Easwaran (trans.), *The Upanishads* (New Delhi: Penguin Books, 1996), Verse 14 from Canto 3, Part I, of *Katha Upanishad*, 89.
9. Dhruv Bhatt, *Tattvamasi* (That Thou Art), translated by Anjani Naravane (New Delhi: Sahitya Akademi, 2008), 52-53.
10. Linda Hess, *Bodies of Song* (New Delhi: Permanent Black, 2015), 79.
11. As quoted in Sy Safransky (ed.), *Sunbeams: A Book of Quotations* (Berkeley: North Atlantic Press, 1990), 67.
12. Rabindranath Tagore, *Gitanjali* (New York: The Macmillan Company, 1920), Verse 14.
13. Coleman Barks (trans.), *The Soul of Rumi: A New Collection of Ecstatic Poems* (San Francisco: HarperOne, 2002).
14. Source: http: / / www.lamrim.com / hhdl / heartsutra.html
15. Anita Barrows, Joanna Macy (trans. & ed.), *In Praise of Mortality: Selections from Rainer Maria Rilke's Duino Elegies and Sonnets to Orpheus* (New York: Riverhead Books, 2005), Ninth Elegy.

ACKNOWLEDGEMENTS

With gratitude to...

Shabnam, founder of the Kabir Project, and a dear friend, colleague and mentor to me personally. Some of the translations in the book are hers and several are ours together (see Individual Translation Credits), and her inputs inform the ideas and writing in this book. She has been an inspiration and a support throughout this incredible journey for me of immersing in the river of song and poetry that has been flowing through this land for centuries.

Smriti Chanchani, Psalm Paul, Prashant Parvatneni and Namrata Karthik at the Kabir Project in Bengaluru, for ever-present and considerable support in the work of preparing this book.

The incredible folk singers and practitioners that I have had the good fortune to encounter and to learn from. Mahesha Ram, Prahlad Tipanya, Parvathy Baul, late Abdullah Hussain Turk, Kaluram Bamaniya, Mukhtiyar Ali, Mavji Jagariya, Omprakash Nayak, Hemant Chauhan, Mooralala Marwada, Mitha Khan and Sumar Kadu, and many, many others. They are the flowing streams keeping the tradition alive.

Kaladhar Mutwa and Asif Rayama in Kutch, Pooja Kaul and Arnab Basu in Bangalore, Gopal Singh Chauhan in Bikaner, and all the folk singers themselves, for extensive research and translation support.

Mazharuddin Mutwa, Farah Naqvi and Arvinder Chamak for help in decoding difficult texts.

Mita Kapur of Siyahi, and Ravi Singh and Yauvanika Chopra of Speaking Tiger for bringing this book to life.

The Srishti Institute of Art, Design and Technology, Bengaluru, for providing a nurturing space and fostering this and other undertakings of the Kabir Project. All of the Kabir Project's works down the years have taken shape at Srishti.

And finally, a deep debt of gratitude to the tradition itself. The poets, the singers, the listeners, the lovers—it is an incredible wealth, an immense treasure, that we are very fortunate to inherit.